WHO GOT GAME?

BASKETBALL

AMAZING BUT TRUE STORIES!

Derrick Barnes

ILLUSTRATED BY **Jez Tuya**

WORKMAN PUBLISHING ★ NEW YORK

TO MY LITTLE CUZZOS

CAMERON (BIGGIE), JUSTIN, AND TYLER

#BarnesBrothersForever —DB

TO MY DARLING WIFE,

JANE.

I LOVE YOU. —JT

- -

WORKMAN KIDS
WORKMAN PUBLISHING
HACHETTE BOOK GROUP, INC.
1290 AVENUE OF THE AMERICAS
NEW YORK, NY 10104
WORKMAN.COM

WORKMAN KIDS IS AN IMPRINT OF WORKMAN PUBLISHING, A DIVISION OF HACHETTE BOOK GROUP, INC.

THE WORKMAN NAME AND LOGO ARE REGISTERED TRADEMARKS OF HACHETTE BOOK GROUP, INC.
DESIGN BY SARA CORBETT, MOLLY MAGNELL, JOHN PASSINEAU, AND KARA STRUBEL
COVER BY SARA CORBETT

THE PUBLISHER IS NOT RESPONSIBLE FOR WEBSITES (OR THEIR CONTENT) THAT ARE NOT OWNED BY THE PUBLISHER.

WORKMAN BOOKS MAY BE PURCHASED IN BULK FOR BUSINESS, EDUCATIONAL, OR PROMOTIONAL USE. FOR INFORMATION,
PLEASE CONTACT YOUR LOCAL BOOKSELLER OR THE HACHETTE BOOK GROUP SPECIAL MARKETS DEPARTMENT
AT SPECIAL.MARKETS@HBGUSA.COM.

LIBRARY OF CONGRESS CATALOGING-IN-PUBLICATION DATA IS AVAILABLE.

ISBN 978-1-5235-0554-8

FIRST EDITION NOVEMBER 2023 APS

DISTRIBUTED IN EUROPE BY HACHETTE LIVRE, 58 RUE JEAN BLEUZEN, 92 178 VANVES CEDEX, FRANCE.
DISTRIBUTED IN THE UNITED KINGDOM BY HACHETTE BOOK GROUP, UK, CARMELITE HOUSE,
50 VICTORIA EMBANKMENT, LONDON EC4Y 0DZ.

PRINTED IN DONGGUAN, CHINA, ON RESPONSIBLY SOURCED PAPER.

10 9 8 7 6 5 4 3 2

CONTENTS

BASKETBALL. B-BALL. HOOPS.

No matter what you call it, the sport has a long history. A Canadian physical education teacher named Dr. James Naismith invented basketball, and the first game tipped off in 1891 in a tiny YMCA in Springfield, Massachusetts. No lie. Today, there are organized leagues of ballers of all ages, all over the planet. More than 250 million people worldwide lace up their sneakers and hoop on neighborhood courts, in school gymnasiums, and in multimillion-dollar arenas, from Boston to Barcelona to Beijing.

You might already know some of basketball's biggest icons and superstars. Many of them go by a single name or initials: Magic, MJ, LeBron, KD, Steph. But this book shines a little bit of light on the ballers, buzzer-beaters, and record-breakers who don't always get the attention they most definitely deserve: like the game's first female hoopers, or the first NBA players and coaches of African American descent. You'll find out about the highest-scoring game in NCAA history, or what exactly a quadruple-double is. Now you *will* know, and everyone around you will, too, because you're going to flex like the ultimate basketball aficionado.

So consider this the tip-off. Let's go!

1

PREMIER PIONEERS

IMPORTANT B-BALL ICONS

Not everyone in this chapter had a sweet jump shot or could dunk from the foul line. But there's no doubt they were all mold–breakers. These hoops pioneers are just a handful of the many important people from all around the world who have helped spread the popularity and mad love for basketball. Each are pillars, foundational pieces, and legends. If you didn't know their names before, you sure will now.

Ever heard of that phrase, "If there wasn't a _____, then there wouldn't be a _____"? These are the names that you may want to insert in the first blank slot. Let's check them out.

THE "AIR"
BEFORE
JORDAN

JULIUS
"DR. J"
ERVING

Before **JULIUS ERVING** laced up his Chuck Taylor sneakers and joined the pros in 1971, dunks were boring. Hard to believe, right? Well, back then, dunks were just another easy, high-percentage way for a tall "big man" (forward or center) to drop the ball through the hoop. No flash, no style, and definitely no 360s, alley-oops, or reverses. A center might stand in the painted area of the court, right beneath the rim, and gently dunk the ball like a tiny, glazed doughnut dipped into a cup of coffee.

But then Julius came along. He added some power and acrobatic artistry, transforming a dunk into a "slam." He even soared in for a slam dunk from as far away as the free throw line, flying like he had a pair of broad, golden wings across his back.

Julius was a good ballplayer at Roosevelt High School in Hempstead, New York, where he earned the nicknames "The Doctor" and "Dr. J." He wasn't recruited by any powerhouse colleges, so in 1968, he enrolled at the University of Massachusetts, which wasn't as famous for its hoops team. But before playing for UMass, Dr. J became a legend at Rucker Park, or "the Rucker"— a world-famous basketball court in Harlem, New York.

Playing above the rim with flair and style was the norm at the Rucker, unlike in the NBA at the time. Dr. J had tremendous leaping ability and crazy athleticism. He commanded that space above the rim like an air traffic controller. He played with force, pride, and a fully rounded Afro hairstyle flowing in the wind. In the early 1970s, when the phrase "I'm Black and I'm proud!" first resonated throughout the African American community, Dr. J would become an instant cultural hero.

At UMass, Erving averaged an outstanding 26.3 points and 20.2 rebounds per game. He decided to go pro and skipped his senior year. But the NBA had a rule that players needed to be at least four years out of high school in order to get drafted. That's when a smaller pro league, the American Basketball Association (ABA), came in.

Players could leave college early and hoop in this exciting new pro league. The ABA had athletic, high-flying players and wild new inventions, like the three-point shot, an annual slam-dunk contest, and a red, white, and blue basketball.

After starring for the Virginia Squires for two seasons, Dr. J was traded to another ABA team, the New York Nets. That's when he really heated up, winning three straight MVP awards and the 1974 and 1976 ABA Championships. Dr. J also won the very first slam-dunk contest, held in 1976 during the ABA All-Star Game. For most hoops fans, that dunk was the first they'd seen made from the free throw line. Jumping to the rim from that far back, he looked like the Statue of Liberty—in sneakers.

DOC'S MOST FAMOUS DUNK

On January 5, 1983, Dr. J shocked the basketball world with one of his signature dunks. His Philadelphia 76ers hosted the LA Lakers, headlined by superstars Magic Johnson and Kareem Abdul-Jabbar. During the game, the ball ricocheted into the air toward the sideline. It bounced once, Doc scooped it up, and then he charged toward the rim. He took flight from the baseline, cradling the ball like a baby. While in midair, he swung the ball in a windmill-type motion and then rocked the rim with authority. It was a thing of beauty, aptly dubbed the "Rock the Cradle" dunk. The more than 18,000 fans in attendance that night at the Spectrum Arena lost their minds!

After the end of the 1976 season, the ABA closed its doors and four of its teams (the Nets, Nuggets, Pacers, and Spurs) joined the NBA. Erving went to the Philadelphia 76ers, where he won the NBA MVP award in 1981 and led the team to its third-ever championship in 1983.

Doc played his entire eleven-season NBA career with Philadelphia. He retired in 1987 with 30,026 points combined from the NBA and ABA. He left the game as a well-respected and iconic superstar. He has influenced every high-floating baller who has followed him, whether they know it or not. Doc was a slam-dunking pioneer.

THE NBA'S FIRST
BLACK PLAYERS

NATHANIEL
"SWEETWATER"
CLIFTON

EARL
LLOYD

CHUCK
COOPER

For a long time, professional basketball lacked anything close to the diversity we see today. Three out of four current NBA players is of African descent, but when the NBA began in 1946, just 150 players filled the rosters for initial teams—and all of them were White.

The very first non-White player was a Japanese American point guard named Wataru "Wat" Misaka. He was drafted by the New York Knicks in 1947, the same year that Jackie Robinson broke the color barrier in Major League Baseball. Even after Misaka and Robinson made history, the country's biases and unwillingness to accept all people as equals—both on and off the court—would not fully go away.

Everything began to change in basketball in 1950, when the NBA welcomed its first three Black players: Nathaniel "Sweetwater" Clifton, Chuck Cooper, and Earl Lloyd. For the most part, their White teammates and coaches treated them fairly. But these iron-willed pros endured terrible racist abuse from White fans, and in some cities they couldn't stay in the same hotels or eat in the same restaurants as the rest of their teams.

Sometimes it's hard to imagine that this behavior happened regularly. But these things did happen—in America, and not so long ago. And it takes fearless, hopeful pioneers to create change. Who were these young "catalysts" who changed the NBA forever?

First up: **NATHANIEL "SWEETWATER" CLIFTON**. While Lloyd and Cooper were great teammates and essential role players, Clifton was a bona fide star. The center/forward made an NBA All-Star team and averaged 10.0 points and 8.2 rebounds per game for his career. The man they called "Sweetwater" (nicknamed for his obsession with soda as a kid) was a multisport athlete, playing both basketball and baseball. He hooped at Xavier University and fought in the army during World War II. After returning home from the war, Sweetwater played with the Harlem Globetrotters, a super-popular, all-Black traveling exhibition basketball team. Then, in 1950, he signed with the New York Knicks, becoming the first undrafted Black player to ever sign a contract with an NBA team.

Clifton played his first NBA contest on November 4, 1950, against the Tri-Cities Blackhawks (today's Atlanta Hawks). The six-foot-seven-inch dazzling scorer enjoyed an eight-year NBA career, including seven seasons with the Knicks and one with the Pistons. He was inducted into the Hall of Fame in 2014 and was also celebrated for his community service in New York City.

In 1950, CHARLES "CHUCK" COOPER became the very first Black player drafted in the history of the league. The Boston Celtics selected the shot-blocking All-American small forward out of Duquesne University in Pittsburgh with the fourteenth selection in the second round. Chuck played his first game on November 1, 1950, with the Celtics against the Pistons.

After a solid rookie year, he had a six-season career, playing for the Celtics, Hawks, and Pistons. He retired in 1956 and became extremely active in his hometown community of Pittsburgh, Pennsylvania, working in education and equal rights. Cooper was inducted into the Naismith Memorial Basketball Hall of Fame in 2019.

EARL LLOYD, nicknamed "The Big Cat," was a defensive-minded, All-American forward from West Virginia State University. He was the second Black player drafted in 1950 when a former NBA team called the Washington Capitols picked him in the ninth round. Although Lloyd was selected at the tail end of the draft, he was actually the first Black man to play a game in the NBA.

On Halloween night, October 31, 1950, Lloyd suited up against the Rochester Royals (today's Sacramento Kings). All of his teammates were White, but they had played on college teams with Black players and welcomed Lloyd as one of their own. The Capitols lost the game, and Mr. Lloyd scored only 6 points. He played just seven more games with Rochester after that.

After serving in the Korean War, Lloyd then played six seasons with the Syracuse Nationals (today's Philadelphia 76ers). He helped them win a championship in 1955, when he became one of the first Black men to play in an NBA Finals game (along with rookie teammate Jim Tucker). Lloyd played two seasons with the Detroit Pistons and then called it quits. He made history again in 1971 by becoming the first Black head coach in the history of the Pistons. In 2003, he was inducted into the Basketball Hall of Fame.

Here's a major salute to these three gentlemen for paving the way for every Black basketball player to set foot onto an NBA court after them. They shone as players, coaches, and icons, both in the game and in their communities.

GEORGE MIKAN

THE GAME'S FIRST GREAT BIG MAN

Gheorghe Mureşan of Romania and Manute Bol of Sudan are listed as the tallest players in NBA history. Both men stood at seven feet, seven inches tall. But long before either one of them hit the court, GEORGE MIKAN was considered the NBA's first real star and its first dominant big man. So much of what defines the center position in today's game—rebounding, shot-blocking, and deadly moves like the hook shot—all started with George Mikan.

Nicknamed "Mr. Basketball," Mikan played in the NBA from 1947 to 1956. He stood at six foot, ten inches, which was mighty tall in pro hoops at the time. Not only was Mikan enormous, but he was also surprisingly agile, athletic, and quick-footed for his height.

Mr. Basketball wasn't always a graceful colossus of the court. As a boy he was shy, a little clumsy, and wore thick, round glasses. He grew up in Joliet, Illinois, and was from a Croatian and Lithuanian immigrant family who owned a popular restaurant. Young George was always the tallest kid in all his elementary school classes. He even hit six feet before he was eleven years old!

In high school, George tried out for the varsity basketball team, but the coach didn't think an extra-tall kid who wore glasses during games could play ball. Big mistake! After George enrolled at DePaul University in Chicago, first-year coach Ray Meyer saw something special in him. Coach Meyer worked with his new freshman giant for more than six weeks. He took him through a tough battery of drills and agility tests until George was light on his feet like a ballerina and his confidence was through the roof.

In one drill, George would make a layup with his left hand, catch the rebound with his right hand, shoot a layup with his right hand, rebound the ball with his left hand, and repeat it over and over. That is now called the Mikan Drill, and nearly every center and forward around the world has practiced it.

Big George became a three-time All-American and two-time College Player of the Year while at DePaul. Opposing teams just couldn't do much to stop him. They couldn't get a shot off without him swatting the ball down like it was a mosquito. Plus, he mastered a nasty left-handed skyhook shot that was unblockable.

After graduating, George led the Chicago Gears of the National Basketball League (NBL) to a championship in 1947. But he is best remembered as being a dominant player in the NBA with the Minneapolis Lakers. (Yep, those same Lakers that now play in Los Angeles.) He led the Lakers to five championships in seven seasons, making them the NBA's first

dynasty team. But because of his big frame and physical style of play in the paint, Mikan suffered a ton of injuries. He retired after the 1955–56 season. He later opened his own law firm in Minneapolis and became the first commissioner of the ABA.

The NBA's first real superstar left a long-lasting legacy of length, height, power, and size. Mikan averaged a whopping 23.1 points and 13.4 rebounds per game. When he left the sport, he was the league's record holder for most points ever, with 11,914. Maybe best of all, he was the very first NBA player inducted into the Basketball Hall of Fame in 1959.

When Mikan passed away in 2005, Shaquille O'Neal—himself a Laker from 1996 to 2004—paid for his hero's funeral expenses. Superstar centers like Shaq, Anthony Davis, Nikola Jokić, and Kareem Abdul-Jabbar owe a ton of respect to the first great center who made it possible for every big fella to dominate the game.

"MUGGSY"

BOGUES

FIVE-FOOT-THREE
AND RISING

As a child, Tyrone Bogues's family called him "Little Ty." But after he started balling at age seven on the hoop outside the Lafayette Court housing projects in Baltimore, Maryland, a new nickname was born.

Tyrone quickly developed a reputation on the court as a defensive headache to taller players . . . and that was pretty much everybody. It didn't matter the grade, team, or school, he was always the smallest guy. But Little Ty used that as motivation to just play harder. He was a leader in his crew of friends, who soon nicknamed him **"MUGGSY" BOGUES** after a character from an old film series called the Bowery Boys. He became an ultra-aggressive defensive player who could easily steal or "mug" the ball from any opponent.

Muggsy honed his ball-handling skills at the local rec center, where he faced some of the best competition in the city. They'd laugh when they saw him step onto the court. He never grew taller than 5'3", even into his NBA days. But it didn't matter to Muggsy.

With an enormous 44-inch vertical jump, the little guy could even dunk. He became a neighborhood superstar and earned respect from the taller players.

By the time he reached Paul Laurence Dunbar High School, Muggsy teamed up with three other local superstars from his neighborhood: Reggie Lewis, David Wingate, and Reggie Williams. Each of them would eventually become NBA ballers. Muggsy was the point guard and team captain of the Dunbar Poets (named after Paul Laurence Dunbar, one of America's greatest scribes). They never lost a game. Check it out: From 1981 to 1983, that squad went 60-0! Some have called them the greatest high school basketball team of all time.

Muggsy went on to play at Wake Forest University and continued blowing the minds of his doubters. By the time he graduated in 1987, he was the all-time leader in the Atlantic Coast Conference (ACC) in steals and assists. Later that year, the Washington Bullets (today's Wizards) made history by drafting the shortest player in NBA history with the twelfth overall pick. After one season in Washington, Bogues went to the NBA's brand-new expansion team, the Charlotte Hornets.

It was in Charlotte that Muggsy became an NBA giant as a part of a formidable trio alongside forward Larry Johnson and center Alonzo Mourning. Muggsy played there for nine years and became one of the greatest and most beloved players on one of the league's most popular teams. Having proven himself as a great passer and stealer, he left Charlotte in 1997 as the team's all-time leader in steals, assists, and minutes played. After four more seasons with the Golden State Warriors and Toronto Raptors, Bogues retired at the end of the 2001 season.

Muggsy once said that he believes that he was born a five-foot-three baby because he never remembers being any other height. But it sure seemed to work out well for him. He used any negative or doubting words as fuel to burn in order to be great. Shout-out to all the other great, diminutive NBA players, like Earl Boykins (5′5″), Spud Webb (5′6″), Nate Robinson (5′9″), and Isaiah Thomas (5′9″).

Who'd ever think that a guy who could barely see over tables as a kid would leave such a great legacy in a sport ruled by behemoths and skyscrapers?
Muggsy Bogues did.

SHE MAKES
THE RULES

SENDA
BERENSON
ABBOTT

Dr. James Naismith changed the world forever when he designed the new sport of basketball in 1891. Soon after, just up the road in Northampton, Massachusetts, another physical education teacher read about Dr. Naismith's game in a newspaper. She got the itch to make plays, too—and to make history.

SENDA BERENSON ABBOTT was the first woman to adapt and remix the rules of basketball, which were originally created for men. Excluding women was hugely unfair and reflected many of the biased attitudes of the time: Before 1893, very few women could play team sports or participate in physical activities for leisure. But Berenson was having none of that.

Abbott was a young Jewish immigrant from Lithuania with a background in gymnastics. In 1892, she introduced this new game called basketball to her female students at Smith College. After they played a few informal contests, Berenson organized the first official all-women's collegiate basketball game on March 22, 1893, in Smith's Alumnae Gymnasium.

Playing with Dr. Naismith's original rules, the freshmen girls faced the older, more experienced sophomores. There were zero guys permitted as spectators. The sophomores won, with a final score of 5–4. (Okay, not quite the high-scoring affair you might see today in the WNBA or NCAA—but there was no more than three dribbles allowed at a time back then!)

Meanwhile, Berenson thought that Naismith's rules needed a little tweaking. After the game, she took suggestions from the players, grabbed her pen and pad, and flipped the script. Her new version of hoops was specifically designed for women.

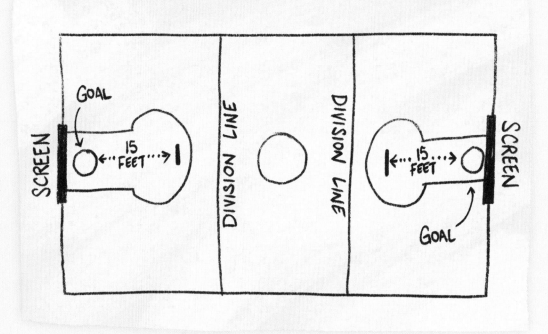

Senda Berenson's Court Diagram

Berenson's rules cut down the number of players on the court for each team from nine to six. (It wasn't a five-on-five game like today.) She also set up three designated zones on the court for players to remain in throughout the entire game. Plus, they could only dribble the ball three times before passing or shooting.

Team cooperation was thoroughly encouraged. As a physical education instructor, Berenson prioritized the health and fitness benefits of basketball for women. The new rules caught on fast at colleges up and down the East Coast. Legions of young women quickly formed teams and small intramural leagues, and a movement was born.

Berenson also helped get the word out about women's basketball by becoming a writer and editor. She wrote riveting articles about the sport and introduced the influential guide *Basket Ball for Women* in 1899. She also later formed and served as the chairwoman for the US Basketball Committee from 1905 to 1917, which set the rules and regulated the sport. Most of the rules that they created stood for more than fifty years.

Berenson is now considered "The Mother of Women's Basketball." Her tenacity and passion for the game is a big reason why young girls all over the world can dream about becoming collegiate hoopers, starring in the WNBA, and playing in the FIBA World Cup or the Olympics. In 1985, Berenson was in the very first group of women inducted into the Naismith Memorial Basketball Hall of Fame. She has also been inducted into the Women's Basketball Hall of Fame and the International Jewish Sports Hall of Fame. Three Hall of Fames!? Now that's clout.

THE NEW YORK RENS

THE MOST DOMINANT BASKETBALL TEAM EVER

What if I were to tell you that one team amassed a ridiculously stellar 2,588-539 record over a twenty-seven-year span? (That's a winning percentage of .855 for my math-heads.) You'd probably think that it was an All-Star squad put together on *NBA 2K*, right? Nope. That real-life team was the **NEW YORK RENAISSANCE**, or Rens.

The Rens were the first professional all–African American team, with all–African American coaching and ownership. The squad was founded in 1923 during a time period called the Harlem Renaissance. It was an exciting and important cultural movement throughout Black America. Tons of notable Black poets, painters, dancers, and playwrights came together in Harlem, New York, where they thrived as artists and thinkers. With the Rens, basketball got a renaissance (which means rebirth) of its own.

The Rens were formed and coached by Robert L. Douglas. A native of Saint Kitts, British West Indies, Douglas put together a team composed of local high school and college All-Stars, as well as some semipros. Coach Douglas then arranged a contract for his squad to play their home games at the Renaissance Ballroom in Harlem.

Get this: The Rens played right on a ballroom floor. Yep. You heard me right! People would show up early to hear local jazz legends perform, watch the Rens defeat an opponent, and then dance all night afterward. The Rens played their first game in 1923, against an all-White team. It was their first of *many* victories.

The Rens also barnstormed, which means they traveled around the country to play games but didn't belong to a league. The Rens beat teams up and down the East Coast and as far west as Kansas City, Missouri. They even played teams down south, where Jim Crow laws were in effect. These were formal and informal rules set up to discriminate against and segregate Black people. The Rens had to eat and sleep at Black-only boardinghouses, churches, and colleges. When traveling, they couldn't make stops at hotels and restaurants, and they even feared for their lives if confronted by hate groups like the Ku Klux Klan or racist townsfolk who didn't think the team belonged in their area.

But do you think a group of ignorant thugs could stop Mr. Douglas's All-Star team? Nope. From 1923 to 1949, they played amateur teams, semipro squads, and some championship-winning professionals like the New York Original Celtics (no relation to today's Boston Celtics). It didn't matter who they faced off against—they whupped them all.

None of the all-White pro basketball leagues of the time allowed the Rens to join their ranks. But the Rens consistently showed that they were better than the rest. In the 1932–33 season, they went on an 88-game winning streak. (The longest NBA streak, by the Lakers, is only 33 games!) In 1939, they won the first-ever World Professional Basketball Tournament, beating the Oshkosh All-Stars 34–25. It was an invitation-only tourney where pro and traveling teams like the Rens competed and reigned supreme.

Despite facing discrimination at every turn, the New York Renaissance were eventually recognized by the greater hoops community. The entire organization was inducted into the Hall of Fame in 1963. Coach Douglas was the first Black person ever inducted into the Hall, in 1972, and five players were later inducted as well. They were: Chuck "Tarzan" Cooper (probably the most popular Rens player ever), William "Pop" Gates (one of basketball's best centers during his time), Nat "Sweetwater" Clifton (one of the first Black ballers to play in the NBA), John Isaacs (the Rens' fiery leader and guard), and Zack Clayton (the team's fiercest defender).

Although there were many other all-Black traveling basketball teams, collectively referred to as the "Black Fives," no other dominated the court like the Renaissance squad from Harlem. Thank you, Coach Douglas, for defying the odds and dunking on Jim Crow and discrimination.

THE BLACK FIVES

Before the NBA integrated in 1950, most of America was heavily segregated and Black athletes weren't allowed to play professional basketball against White players. But from 1904 to 1950, there was a collective of traveling all–Black teams called the "Black Fives" who were some of the best basketball squads of all time.

Named for the five players on the court for each team, this was basketball's equivalent to the Negro Leagues in baseball, which was never one unified league. But the players who came from these teams were great—and many would have been superstars if they were allowed to play in the NBA or other White pro leagues.

Some of the best teams included the INDEPENDENT PLEASURE CLUB (New Jersey), the LOS ANGELES RED DEVILS, the SAVOY BIG FIVE (Chicago), the WASHINGTON (DC) BEARS, the ALPHA PHYSICAL CULTURE CLUB (Harlem), and the SECOND STORY MORRYS (Pittsburgh). They produced tons of legends, such as Clarence "Fats" Jenkins, Ulysses Young, Archie Thomas, Albert "Runt" Pullins, and pretty much all the dudes from the mighty Rens that you read about earlier. There were at least twenty prominent teams from that era that barnstormed. They traveled on the road to face other Black-owned teams in front of excited, all-Black crowds. Between 1907 and 1925, those teams battled it out for the Colored Basketball World's Championship.

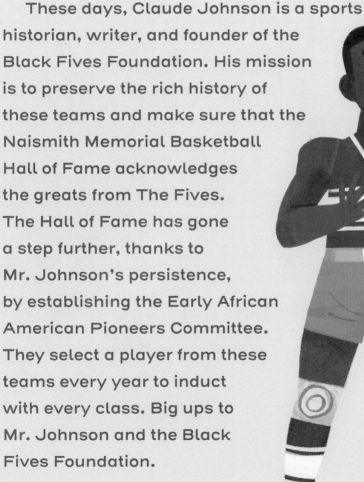

These days, Claude Johnson is a sports historian, writer, and founder of the Black Fives Foundation. His mission is to preserve the rich history of these teams and make sure that the Naismith Memorial Basketball Hall of Fame acknowledges the greats from The Fives. The Hall of Fame has gone a step further, thanks to Mr. Johnson's persistence, by establishing the Early African American Pioneers Committee. They select a player from these teams every year to induct with every class. Big ups to Mr. Johnson and the Black Fives Foundation.

DICK VITALE

THE VOICE OF COLLEGE BASKETBALL

If you've ever tuned in to ESPN to check out the best NCAA basketball game of the week, odds are strong that you've heard the voice of one memorable commentator: **DICK VITALE**. If so, then you've also heard some of the most colorful and creative basketball lingo ever created.

Words alone can't define how important Dick Vitale has been to college basketball culture in America. Before him, sports commentators—particularly in college hoops—were a bit boring, as if they were reporting the news. Not Dickie V! He became a college basketball ambassador with his brand of colorful, catchy, excitable banter. Once you've heard him broadcast a big game between rivals like the Duke Blue Devils versus the Maryland Terrapins or the Michigan Wolverines versus the Michigan State Spartans, you'll never look at NCAA basketball the same. Vitale's energy, voice, and mere presence at a game makes any college hoops experience feel like a major event.

Vitale was born in East Rutherford, New Jersey, in 1939 to a working-class Italian American family. Before he ever entered the broadcast booth, Vitale honed his basketball chops as a successful coach. He got started early at age twenty-four, becoming a head coach at Garfield High School in New Jersey for one season. The next year, he returned to his alma mater and began a super-successful run as coach of East Rutherford High.

At East Rutherford, between 1964 and 1971, he led his teams to a 131-47 overall record and two state titles. He made such a big name for himself that he kept climbing the basketball-coaching ladder. In 1973, he became the head honcho at the University of Detroit, leading that squad to the 1977 NCAA tournament and a 78-30 overall record. The guy was a winner every single place he went! That is . . . until he got to the highest level: the NBA.

In one year with the Detroit Pistons in 1978–79, his record was an abysmal 30-52 and he was soon let go.

Vitale soon received a call from a TV executive named Scotty Connal from a brand-new cable sports network called ESPN. Connal liked the energy that Dickie V exhibited up and down the court while coaching games.

But Vitale wasn't sure what he was getting into. A channel broadcasting sports and nonstop highlights all day long? Who would watch that? (If he only knew!)

Thinking it was just a quick job before landing his next coaching position, Dickie V agreed to be a commentator on the network's first-ever college basketball game. On December 5, 1979, only three months after ESPN opened for business, Vitale called the action between the Wisconsin Badgers and the DePaul Blue Demons. A star was born. Vitale soon became a pillar of the network, which now has multiple channels and websites, broadcasts to tens of millions, and is worth more than $50 billion. Dickie V has been there for it all, and he has most definitely been an integral part of the network's college basketball success.

Over the years, Vitale has had his own shows on ESPN and written bestselling books on all things basketball. He has also been extremely active in raising money for cancer research. Vitale was inducted into the Naismith Memorial Basketball Hall of Fame and the College Basketball Hall of Fame in 2008. The voice, the energy, the basketball wisdom, the philanthropy, the imaginative lexicon—that's Dick Vitale, and it ain't even close.

DICKIE V'S BIG-GAME PHRASES

★ **P.T.P.** — a primetime player; a superstar

★ **DIAPER DANDY** — an outstanding freshman player

★ **DOUGHNUT OFFENSE** — a team without a good player at the center position

★ **TRIFECTA** — a game-winning or game-altering three-point shot

★ **HIGH RISER** — a player with hops who can practically jump out of the gym

★ **SPACE EATER** or **HUMAN SPACESHIP** — a big player, like a power forward or a center

★ **DIPSY-DOO** or **DUNK-A-ROO** — a flashy slam dunk

★ **KNEE-KNOCKER** — a close game

★ **WILSON SANDWICH** — when your shot is rejected in your face (named after Wilson basketballs)

★ **ALL-WINDEX TEAM** — a team full of players who clean the glass (are great rebounders)

★ **ALL-AT&T TEAM** — a team full of great long-distance shooters

★ **ALL-INNOVATIVE TEAM** — a team with great point guards

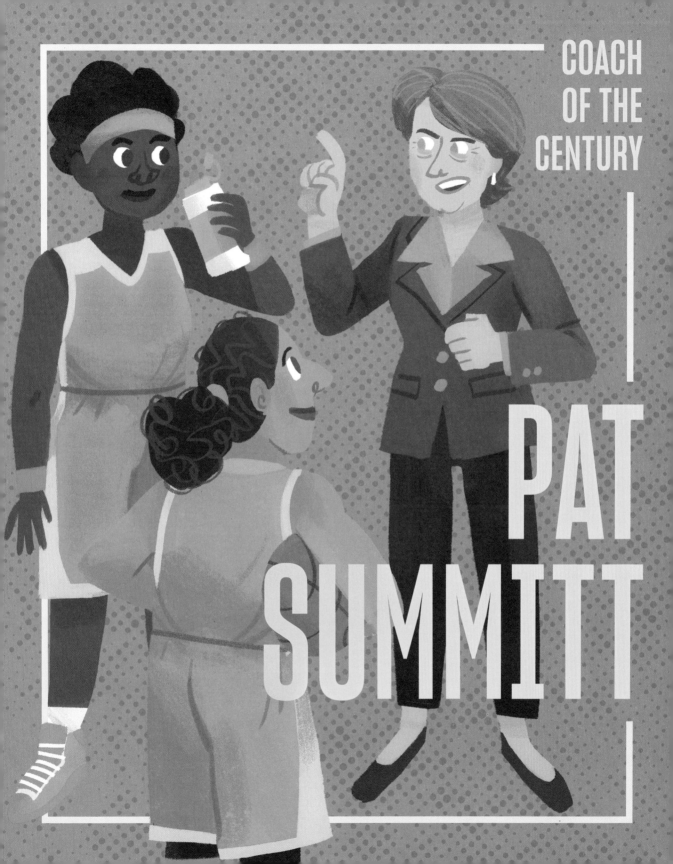

COACH OF THE CENTURY

PAT SUMMITT

On March 17, 2018, in the second round of the 2018 NCAA tournament, legendary Duke head coach Mike "Coach K" Krzyzewski (pronounced shih-ZHEF-skee) made history by winning his 1,099th game. It was the most wins in Division I basketball history—an incredible accomplishment. But who was the coach who had notched 1,098 victories and was named the Naismith Coach of the Century in 2000? Meet PAT SUMMITT, one of the greatest coaches in all of sports history. Not too bad for a farmgirl from Henrietta, Tennessee.

Born Patricia Sue Head, she grew up playing basketball with her brothers in the barn on her parents' dairy farm. All of the three Head boys were good athletes and each earned scholarships to play various sports in college. Pat was also an excellent high school baller, but the world of college sports was very different for female students during that time. When she graduated from high school in 1970, there were no scholarships given to girls who were superb athletes, and Pat's parents had to pay for her education.

Summitt became a Lady Pacer at the University of Tennessee at Martin, and her journey as a basketball lifer began. She soon racked up some big-time accomplishments in international play: She won a silver medal in the very first World University Games in 1973, a gold medal in the 1975 Pan American Games, and a silver medal in the 1976 Summer Olympics in Montreal.

But even during her successful playing career, Summitt got bit by the coaching bug. After she took a job as a coaching assistant at the University of Tennessee in 1974, her big break came when the head coach abruptly quit. Twenty-two-year-old Pat Summitt took over. She won her first game, 69–32, on January 10, 1975, against Middle Tennessee State. Little did she know there'd be more than a thousand wins to come.

It took Summitt only five seasons to win her hundredth game in 1979. She won her first Southeastern Conference (SEC) championship in 1980, and, in 1984, Summitt returned to the Olympics. She became the first person—man or woman—to both play for and coach US Olympic basketball. Her squad won the gold medal for the first time in US Olympic Women's team history. On March 29, 1987, Summitt finally led her Lady Vols to the school's first NCAA title by whupping Louisiana Tech, 67–44. Championships soon became a habit.

THE PASSING OF TITLE IX

Two years before Summitt became head coach of the Tennessee Vols, the US Congress passed Title IX, in 1972, one of the country's most important federal civil rights laws ever. It states that all colleges receiving money from the government—which is most of them in the United States—must provide fair and equal treatment of all students in all areas, including athletics.

Before the Title IX law, very few schools funded sports programs for female students, and the NCAA hadn't acknowledged any women's sports at all. Only one in twenty-seven young women played a collegiate sport—now it's about two in five. Talk about a big and necessary jump. Today, women's basketball, soccer, gymnastics, and track and field are some of the most popular collegiate sports in the country.

Summitt led Tennessee to the mountaintop again in 1989, 1991, 1996–98 (an incredible three-peat), 2007, and, finally, in 2008, for a ridiculous total of eight titles. In 2009, Summitt won her thousandth game, against the Lady Bulldogs of Georgia, making her the first Division I coach to reach the thousand mark. (She was also the first women's coach to be paid over $1 million per season.) Coach Summitt took her teams to the Final Four eighteen times and earned NCAA Coach of the Year honors five times (1987, 1989, 1994, 1998, and 2004). She never, *ever* had a losing season as a coach. Dig that.

Coach Summitt's legendary coaching style was centered in fairness and personal responsibility required of each and every player. She believed in genuine, constructive criticism and praise. She put an emphasis on her players building a strong work ethic, having self-discipline, and putting the team first. Her graduation rate for the thirty-eight years of coaching? One hundred percent. That's right, every single player graduated—maybe that's her most impressive coaching stat.

Summitt's last game coaching was on April 18, 2012, in the Elite 8 round of the NCAA tournament. Tragically, on June 28, 2016, Coach Summitt passed away from Alzheimer's disease. Her legacy as a winner, as the ultimate motivator, and as a leader espousing education is what she'll be remembered for best. She was inducted into the Women's Basketball Hall of Fame in 1999, the Naismith Memorial Basketball Hall of Fame in 2000, the Tennessee Women's Hall of Fame in 2011, and the International Basketball Federation (FIBA) Hall of Fame in 2013.

Salute to a true coaching giant and the greatest Tennessee Vol of all time.

WAYNE EMBRY

THE FIRST BLACK GM IN THE NBA

Major League Baseball didn't have its first Black general manager, Bill Lucas of the Atlanta Braves, until 1976. It took the NFL until 2002 to do it, when Hall of Fame tight end Ozzie Newsome filled the position for the Baltimore Ravens. (Let me say that again—2002!) But in the NBA, the Milwaukee Bucks were trailblazers.

WAYNE EMBRY wasn't always a business-minded suit-and-tie guy. Oh no. He could ball, too. As a matter of fact, the 6'8" center's on-court nickname was "The Wall" because it was so hard to make a shot on the man. He played in the NBA for eleven years with the Cincinnati Royals, Boston Celtics, and Milwaukee Bucks. He was a five-time All-Star and even won a championship with the Celtics in 1968. He retired the following season and then took a position in the Bucks' management. He started as an assistant manager and later became the director of player personnel. In 1972, the Bucks promoted him again, and Mr. Embry became the first Black general manager in the history of the NBA and all major American sports.

As a member of the front office—the people calling the shots for the team—he influenced the decision to bring in one of his ex-teammates, Hall of Fame point guard Oscar Robertson. The Bucks matched the "Big O" up with their first-round pick, UCLA wonder-kid Kareem Abdul-Jabbar, and won their first championship in the 1970–71 season.

Mr. Embry held the GM spot in Milwaukee for seven years. Since then, he's also been the head honcho for the Cleveland Cavaliers and Toronto Raptors. He even took home the Executive of the Year Award twice: in 1992 and 1998, for his role in turning the Cavaliers into real contenders. The Hall of Famer has served as both the GM and senior advisor for the Raptors since 2004.

With an overwhelming sixty years in a variety of roles in

IT TAKES TWO TO MAKE A THING GO RIGHT

GREATEST DYNAMIC DUOS

★ **"THE BIG FUNDAMENTAL"** and **"POP"**— **Tim Duncan** spent his entire nineteen-year career with coach **Gregg Popovich**'s San Antonio Spurs. In that span, Duncan won Rookie of the Year, MVP, and Finals MVP, and made fifteen All-Star appearances, while Pop won Coach of the Year three times. Most important, they won five NBA Championships together.

★ **CELTICS DYNASTY**— During their seven seasons as teammates, **Bob Cousy** won one MVP award while **Bill Russell** won four. They won six NBA titles between the 1957 and 1963 seasons. Bill Russell was also extremely active in civil rights for African professional basketball, Mr. Embry has seen it all and done it all. This Black man from Springfield, Ohio, has lived through the civil rights movement, Jim Crow laws, and all kinds of discrimination. He has personally witnessed the advancements and triumphs of people of color both inside and outside sports. And he's been a strong mentor and source of inspiration for others who aspire to land leadership roles in professional sports, regardless of their race or gender.

Americans. Bob Cousy, although a team captain, regretted decades later that he never stood with and fought for his Black teammates. They were outstanding teammates, but that lack of public support kept them from ever becoming close friends.

★ **"SHOWTIME LAKERS"**— Talk about a super Hall of Fame Duo. In 1979, after leading Michigan State to a Men's National Championship, **Earvin "Magic" Johnson** was drafted by the LA Lakers and helped lead the team to another title. But he didn't do it alone. He joined forces with the second-leading scorer of all time, center **Kareem Abdul-Jabbar.** Together they ruled the NBA in the 1980s with their fast-paced "showtime" brand of ball. The two co-led Los Angeles to five championships.

CHAPTER 2

SENSATIONAL STORIES

RARE ROUNDBALL REPORTS AND TALES

The basketball world has long celebrated (and occasionally exaggerated) amazing athletic feats and antics by players from both on and off the court. There's a lot of truth and a little bit of lore surrounding bold championship predictions, tales from iconic basketball courts, and literal and figurative ankle breaking. But in this beloved sport, one thing is for sure: These legendary players and teams have enriched the vast history of the game. Let's take a look at some pretty wild and amazing "nothing but net" narratives.

SPENCER HAYWOOD'S
FIGHT TO GO PRO

FROM THE BASKETBALL COURT TO THE SUPREME COURT

In the late 1960s, the NBA wouldn't draft players unless they were four years out of high school. That meant they needed to either go to college or find some other way to play hoops until they were old enough. It was a very different time from more recent years, when superstars like Devin Booker, Jayson Tatum, and Joel Embiid entered the league after just one year of college. But one super-talented player challenged the NBA's rule—and won.

SPENCER HAYWOOD, a six-foot-eight power forward at the University of Detroit, thought it was absurd that the NBA denied him the right to go pro. After all, he had even competed as a member of the gold medal–winning 1968 Olympic basketball team! After his sophomore season at Detroit, the 19-year-old star athlete signed with the Denver Rockets of the rival American Basketball Association (ABA), which welcomed young players. In the 1969–70 season, Haywood led the league in rebounds (19.5) and scoring (30.0) and won the MVP award.

Soon enough, the NBA's Seattle SuperSonics (today's Thunder) took notice of the young star and offered Spencer a contract, even though he was still just three years out of high school. The NBA blocked the signing, so in 1971, Spencer took them to a different kind of court—the United States Supreme Court. The judges ruled in Spencer's favor, and the NBA allowed him to play for the Sonics. Over the course of a Hall of Fame career, Haywood made four All-Star teams and won wa championship in 1980 with the Lakers.

Don't get it twisted: Most NBA players would encourage student-athletes to finish their college degrees. But many of the best superstars, like Haywood, choose to join the pros early so they can earn a living from their exceptional talents. To this day, NCAA athletes still aren't paid salaries, and many players and commentators think that this is grossly unfair. No matter how you slice it, Spencer Haywood was a pioneer who stood up for young athletes and their right to make the money they deserved. He paved the way for generations of NBA players who came after him.

SIX GREAT NBA PLAYERS OUT OF HIGH SCHOOL

1. **KEVIN GARNETT** `1995` One-time champion, 15-time All-Star, Hall of Famer
2. **KOBE BRYANT** `1996` Five-time champion, 18-time All-Star, Hall of Famer
3. **TRACY MCGRADY** `1997` Seven-time All-Star, Hall of Famer
4. **AMAR'E STOUDEMIRE** `2002` Six-time All-Star, Rookie of the Year
5. **LEBRON JAMES** `2003` Four-time champion, four-time MVP, all-time scoring champ
6. **DWIGHT HOWARD** `2004` One-time champion, eight-time All-Star

CLIP 'EM!

In the middle of March, a basketball coach from a small, little-known college walks out onto a freshly waxed, glistening basketball court. His star point guard follows him onto the hardwood. The court is the centerpiece of a brand-new sports arena that can seat more than 22,000 rowdy college basketball fans. It's just a few hours before a single-game elimination championship match against a "blue-blood" team (a powerhouse college squad that has won multiple titles). The coach and the player stride to the half-court line and face the rim:

COACH: Kid, it's not about the cameras or the screaming fans. . . . Heck, it's not even about that trophy.

TEAM CAPTAIN: Then what's it about, coach?

COACH: [pointing toward the backboard and rim while his voice trembles] It's all about those nets. I want you to bring me those nets when that clock hits zero. All I want are those nets!

This scene (or something very much like it) occurs all across the country during basketball season. Especially at big-time high school playoff games, Amateur Athletic Union (AAU) tournaments, and, of course, the biggest dance of them all: the NCAA Division I championship game. The ritual of the winning team cutting down the net, piece by piece, has become just as important as the trophy presentation. So, how'd it all start?

Legend has it that the post-game ceremony of snipping the nets began at high schools in the Hoosier State. Since the 1920s, Indiana has received the credit for starting the tradition during its famous state high school tournament, the oldest in the country. Mr. Everett "Casey" Case, one of Indiana's most successful high school coaches of all time, cut a few nets down himself during his storied career. He finished his twenty-three years as a high school basketball guru with a jaw-dropping

726-75 record. Case cut down the nets for most of his career as the four-time state championship coach of the Frankfort Hot Dogs (that's right—the Hot Dogs!) between 1922 and 1942.

Case then coached the NC State Wolfpack from 1946 to 1964 and brought Indiana's net-cutting ritual right along with him. After he carried the Wolfpack to their first conference title in 1947, he asked the North Carolina kids to hoist him up. Then he pulled a trusty pair of scissors out of his pocket like a magician and meticulously snipped off the net, piece by piece. No one there had ever seen anything like it before.

Today, there is a protocol in college hoops. After the clock hits zero, the NCAA will provide the winning team with official scissors. Each member of the team gets to climb the official NCAA ladder and snip off a souvenir for themselves. The participants go in order: freshmen to seniors; then coaches; and, finally, the head coach, who usually takes what's left.

Does it seem kind of dangerous for overexcited yet exhausted kids to climb a wobbly ladder on a slippery wooden floor while holding a pair of scissors in their hands? Sure it does. (*Do not try this at home!*) A few coaches have even cut themselves, but to many of them it's well worth the risk. It's a way of saying, "We came. We saw. We conquered . . . and we'll take a little bit of the hoop right along with us!"

THE DAY DAVID SHOOK GOLIATH

ALLEN IVERSON
TAKES MJ'S ANKLES

On March 12, 1997, the defending-champion Chicago Bulls faced the lowly Philadelphia 76ers for the third time that season. The Bulls charged in with a fearsome 54-8 record, and the Sixers were just 16-45. But Philly had a sliver of hope in the form of ALLEN IVERSON, a twenty-one-year-old rookie who happened to be the number-one overall pick in the 1996 NBA draft. Dribbling history would be made that night.

The Sixers had won three championships in its history, but its most recent title had come many years before, in the 1982–83 season. In drafting the young point guard from Georgetown University, they hoped to bring an end to their losing ways. Known by his initials, AI, Allen Iverson's other nickname was "The Answer." So, what was the question? Something like, "How are the 76ers going to win some games for a change?!"

Meanwhile, the Bulls had won four championships within the past six seasons and were led by super-duper-star **MICHAEL JORDAN**, who many people still consider the G.O.A.T.— Greatest of All Time. For Chicago, the game was just a blip on the road map as they cruised to their fifth title. But many thought this face-off between MJ and AI signified an eventual changing of the guard. One iconic play ended up capturing the transition.

Jordan had already cemented himself as the face of the NBA. He was the ideal pitchman for every and any product on Earth. (You might be wearing a Jordan T-shirt or pair of sneakers right now!) Jordan portrayed a clean-cut, hard-working image—and he performed feats that basketball fans had never seen before.

Then along came Iverson, who was nothing like Jordan in his public image. He had a brash personality and a scrappy playing style. He was much shorter, too: only six feet tall to Jordan's six foot six. Where Jordan belonged to the old world of playing golf and wearing custom-made suits, Iverson represented a new generation of athletes from the urban core of America. With his baggy basketball shorts and gold chains, AI was an ambassador of hip-hop culture and a trendsetter of street style. Along with his hip-hop swag came a new style of play, one that centered around having the sickest ball-handling skills imaginable.

His signature move? The crossover, a dribbling fake-out that caught Mike quite by surprise that night in Philly. In the fourth quarter, "The Answer" had the ball at the top of the key. Though Jordan would usually "D-up," or defend, the other team's shooting guard, legendary Bulls coach Phil Jackson directed Jordan to take the young point guard this time around.

Iverson finessed the ball from left to right. Jordan, an elite defender, followed his movements. AI proceeded to bounce the ball between his legs at lightning speed and then hold it as far left as possible. Then, the famous crossover: His Airness fell for it and followed the ball left, freezing just long enough for AI to bring it back to the right. That move freed up Iverson to take a shot, a twenty-foot jumper that he hit with ease.

The crowd went nuts, and the clip has been played millions of times over on sports shows and on YouTube for all eternity. But, alas—it wasn't enough. Though the game was close, the Chicago Bulls won 108 to 104 and went on to become the eventual 1996–97 NBA Champs.

Even so, kids all across the country wanted the kind of golden handles their new idol, Allen Iverson, showed off every night. In total, Iverson and Jordan faced off against each other thirteen times in their NBA careers. Jordan won seven of them and finished his Hall of Fame career with six championships. Iverson, also a Hall of Famer, never reached the promised land of an NBA championship. But MJ will never live down the day that "The Answer" shook him out of his Hanes underwear.

THE RUCKER

THE MOST LEGENDARY BASKETBALL PARK IN AMERICA

"EACH ONE, TEACH ONE."

This was the motto of New York City native, World War II vet, community servant, and neighborhood superstar Holcombe Rucker. He grew up in dire poverty, quit school in the tenth grade, joined the army, and later earned his high school degree upon completing his military service. When Rucker returned to NYC, he wanted recreational basketball to motivate the youth of Harlem, an enormously important center of African American cultural life. The legendary RUCKER PARK would soon be born.

In 1946, Rucker began a sixteen-year-long career as a playground director for the Department of Parks and Recreation in New York City. At the same time, he developed a basketball tournament through the local community center and gained a ton of respect for his work as an advocate for educating the city's kids. By 1954, Rucker's tournament had become one of the most anticipated sporting events on the streets of New York. He organized high school and college divisions and encouraged the participants to keep their grades up and be good citizens in their schools and communities.

The most ingenious element of the tournament was Rucker's addition of games between professionals and streetball stars. All levels of players showed up to test their skills: amateurs from all over the city, college stars, pros from regional or all-Black leagues, and even the handful of Black NBA players at the time. (Remember, Black players weren't allowed to join the NBA until 1950.)

In 1965, the tournament moved to its current location, where the court is a sacred ground on Frederick Douglass Boulevard and West 155th Street in Harlem. The park would be renamed after the great Holcombe Rucker. The Rucker boasted the ultimate streetball experience and became known as the "Mecca" of city basketball. People would sit on the ledges of the buildings

overlooking the court, risking life and limb, to catch a glimpse of the latest star.

Players at the Rucker prized creativity, swagger, and, most of all, wildly acrobatic dunks that the NBA still frowned upon.

The colorful and high-flying play that defines the NBA today takes many of its cues from the style birthed right there at the Rucker. In fact, Rucker Park became a breeding ground of future college and NBA legends like Kareem Abdul-Jabbar, Julius "Dr. J" Erving, Nate "Tiny" Archibald, and Wilt Chamberlain.

But after Holcombe Rucker's untimely passing due to lung cancer at age thirty-nine in 1965, the number of pro players coming out of his courts slowed down for a time. Fortunately, a rebirth of the Mecca occurred in 1982, thanks to a Harlem native and former rapper named Greg Marius, who fused hip-hop with basketball at Rucker Park and created the Entertainers Basketball Classic (EBC). New generations of local, college, and NBA stars have blessed the courts: guys like Rafer "Skip 2 My Lou" Alston, Allen Iverson, Stephon Marbury, Kobe Bryant, Kevin Durant, and Kyrie Irving. What's really cool is that rappers and music industry big shots, like Fat Joe, Diddy, and Jay-Z, created teams to compete in the classic.

Today, NBA and college stars still show up and play at least one game of hoops to test their mettle. And best of all, Holcombe Rucker's passion for enriching Harlem with basketball has inspired summer leagues all over the country that focus on community and education.

GLASS-SHATTERING
DUNKS

BACKBOARDS
GET AN UPGRADE

Has there ever been an NBA player with a more delightful—and intimidating—nickname than that of legendary Philadelphia 76ers center DARRYL DAWKINS? That's right, we're talking about "Chocolate Thunder," baby. Of course, "Chocolate" referred to the color of his skin. But the "Thunder" part came from the sound when his booming, one- or two-handed "tomahawk" jams shook the arena, frightened the innocent, and shattered the backboard like a bazillion broken hearts.

So what's the story with backboards, anyway? Well, glass backboards were first used in 1917. Before that, they were made of wood and looked like little floating walls. Much later,

pro ballers began to get a lot bigger and taller. During the 1970s, gameplay shifted to the zone above the rim. That's when dunks, the main culprit behind shattered backboards, became more common. The first player to bring an NBA backboard down in pieces was a guy named **GUS "HONEYCOMB" JOHNSON**, who

AKA OTHER AWESOME PLAYER NICKNAMES

What would an NBA star be without a really cool nickname? My favorite of all time is simple: Earvin "Magic" Johnson. His passing abilities and leadership were mesmerizing. Here's a list of some other really cool ones. What would your nickname be on the court?

★ GIANNIS ANTETOKOUNMPO—"The Greek Freak"

★ CLYDE DREXLER— "The Glide"

★ PHIL JACKSON— "The Zen Master"

earned the nickname because his game was so sweet. At 6'6" and 230 pounds, "Honeycomb" Johnson was a powerful stalk of an athlete with the elegance of a deer. He played for eleven years in the NBA and was a five-time All-Star. In that time, he dunked and shattered at least three glass backboards. But Chocolate Thunder was the dude who caused the NBA to make big changes.

Within a span of four weeks during the 1979–80 season, Dawkins completely obliterated two backboards in games against the Kansas City Kings and San Antonio Spurs.

★ JASON WILLIAMS — "White Chocolate"

★ GEORGE GERVIN — "The Iceman"

★ BILL BRADLEY — "Dollar Bill"

★ CEDRIC CEBALLOS — "The Garbage Man"

★ KAWHI LEONARD — "The Claw"

★ KEVIN GARNETT — "The Big Ticket"

★ DENNIS RODMAN — "The Worm"

★ BOB COUSY — "Houdini of the Hardwood"

★ KEVIN DURANT — "The Slim Reaper"

Both incidents were spectacles that sent players ducking and running for cover from the explosive cascades of glass pouring onto the hardwood floor. Dawkins named every one of his dunks like they were his children: the Rim-Wrecker, the Look Out Below, the Spine Chiller Supreme, the Yo Mama, and so many more. But the NBA had a name for all those broken backboards: Enough Is Enough!

The league found out that it took 625 pounds of power coming down on the rim to shatter the boards. They started fining Dawkins $5,000 for every fiberglass backboard he damaged. Still, with more and more big guys soaring through the air and pummeling the goal like modern-day giants, something more had to change.

The year before Dawkins's fateful 1979–80 season, the NCAA had attached a magnificent, game-changing invention to their backboards: the breakaway rim. Unlike fixed rims, breakaway rims are designed to withstand the force of dunking. The new equipment had a downward hinge and a spring that allowed the rim to bounce back up. It did wonders to cut down on shattered backboards, increasing the safety of everyone on the court.

The NBA and NCAA would also replace the glass in backboards with a material called plexiglass, or acrylic, which is softer and can better absorb the force of a dunk. As athletes and sports continue to evolve, so must the equipment they use. Today's NBA backboards are made up of a half-inch of special glass with an aluminum frame. And just like that, no more shattered backboards. Chocolate Thunder was the last to do it, but don't forget about good ol' "Shaq Diesel." In his rookie season in 1992–93, **SHAQUILLE O'NEAL** caused the entire goal to buckle and collapse on a ferocious slam for the Orlando Magic. Some big fellas never learn!

AERIAL EXCELLENCE

Can't get enough dunks? We've got you covered. Here's a list of dunks from the NBA Slam Dunk Contest that really took some out-of-the-box thinking:

1 SERGE IBAKA'S STUFFED ANIMAL 2011

Oklahoma City Thunder power forward Serge Ibaka ran from behind the goal, cupped the ball, and dunked it with authority. Not so unusual, right? Wrong. He did it all while grabbing a stuffed animal attached to the rim—and using his teeth to do it. To top it all off, after the dunk, he handed the bear to a kid. Serge is also the first player in NBA history drafted from the Republic of the Congo. My man can speak four languages fluently: Lingala (a Bantu dialect from Africa), English, Spanish, and French.

2 VINCE CARTER'S "IT'S OVER" SLAM 2000

Many basketball experts consider Vince Carter (aka "Vinsanity") to be the greatest dunk artist of all time. The dunk that won it all in 2000 is simply known as "It's Over" because that's what Vince mouthed to the camera after performing the feat. Before the slam, he eyed the rim like a tiger (or a raptor, since he played for Toronto at the time) and then took off toward the hoop. Vince caught the ball in midair off a bounce from his teammate, took it between his legs with both hands, and then completed a vicious windmill slam.

3 DEE BROWN'S "NO-LOOK" DUNK 1991

At a relatively small 6'1", Boston Celtics point guard Dee Brown was an electric jumper. For this contest-winning dunk, he started at half-court, made three simple dribbles, drove to the goal, and took off from inside the free throw circle. Holding the ball in his left hand, he shielded his eyes with his right forearm to obstruct his own view and record the first no-look dunk. (Was Dee Brown dabbing more than thirty years ago?!)

4 BLAKE GRIFFIN'S CAR DUNK 2011

This contest winner was by Los Angeles Clippers power forward and booming rim-rocker Blake Griffin, with some help from his starting point guard, Baron Davis.

Not to mention a full gospel choir and a 2011 Kia Optima that added some theatrics to the stunt! As the choir sang "I Believe I Can Fly," Blake backed up and then came surging full speed toward the hood of the brand-new car. Baron's head appeared out of the sunroof, and as Blake flew over the windshield of the car, Baron popped the ball up through the roof like a slice of bread out of a toaster. The choir sang on as Blake came crashing down on the rim with both hands and landed victorious on the hood.

BONUS DUNK · THE "BUG ON A WINDSHIELD" 2019

In the tiny town of Hammond, Louisiana, a 5'9" guard named Marlain Veal created a dunk called "Bug on the Windshield." The feat took a crew of six other people to pull it off. Two of them helped catapult Marlain, who leaped over the heads of three others. The sixth person threw up the ball right on time for Marlain to jam with both hands. He held tight to the rim and then put his feet on the backboard, just like a bug on the windshield while you're driving down the freeway. There were no giant wiper blades to swat him off, though. That would've been cool!

TATTOO GUARANTEED

"THE JET" INKS A CHAMPIONSHIP TROPHY

Dallas Mavericks guard **JASON "THE JET" TERRY** not only made a bold prediction about his team's Finals performance, but he also sealed the deal with a prophetic tattoo.

One day before a preseason game, veteran Mavericks guard DeShawn Stevenson invited friends and teammates over to his crib to hang out and talk about the upcoming 2010–11 season. The big topic that year was the newly formed Miami Heat super-squad spearheaded by LeBron James. LeBron had taken his talents from Cleveland to South Beach, joining his best friend, superstar guard Dwyane Wade. They had also convinced

All-Star forward Chris Bosh to come over to Miami from the Toronto Raptors, forming one of the fiercest trios of players ever assembled. The Heat were favorites to win the East that year, and LeBron and his crew predicted up to *eight* championships.

But Jason Terry said, "Not so fast." He boldly declared that the Dallas Mavericks would win the Western Conference and then become World Champions—not the Heat. He was so sure that he decided to ink the Larry O'Brien Trophy on the inside of his bicep. Terry's Dallas teammates thought the Jet was nuts! Plus, though he was important to the team, Terry wasn't even a starter. The squad was stacked with point guard Jason Kidd, forward Caron Butler, center Tyson Chandler, forward Shawn "The Matrix" Marion, and former MVP Dirk Nowitzki, who led the team. All were either All-Stars or Olympic gold-medal winners.

Sure enough, at the end of the season, the Mavericks had an impressive 57-25 record and finished third in the Western Conference. In the playoffs, they managed to beat the Portland Trail Blazers, Los Angeles Lakers, and the talented young Oklahoma City Thunder to win the Western Conference. Meanwhile, across the country, the Heat finished with a nearly identical record of 58-24. They won the Eastern Conference and were finally on a collision course with Jason Terry and the Mavs.

The two teams had clashed just five years earlier in the 2005–06 Finals, when Dwyane Wade and Shaquille O'Neal led the Heat over the Mavs, four games to two. Terry and Nowitzki were the only two players still left over from that Dallas team. So revenge may have been a hidden motivation for Jason. You couldn't really tell early on in the series though. He was shooting cold, missing way too many of his three-pointers.

After the coaching staff did a better job of getting him open, the Jet finally took off. In Games 5 and 6, Jason scored an impressive 48 points combined. He hit eight three-pointers after Game 2 and even led the Mavs in scoring during Game 6. They won the series 4-2 and took home the championship trophy as well. Jason Terry flexed that tatted right bicep next to the real thing in front of every camera that he could find, and audiences saw him as a future-seeing, title-winning baller. A fast-breaking fortune-teller, if you will.

Terry believed in himself, believed in his team, and did what a lot of us should do more often: Trust in our abilities without fear until we are victorious.

KEVIN WARE'S UNFORTUNATE BREAK

THE MOST GRUESOME BASKETBALL INJURY EVER

And then there were eight. The University of Louisville men's team finished their 2012–13 season with a 35-5 record and reached the "Elite 8" round of the NCAA tournament for the second season in a row. On March 31, 2013, the Louisville Cardinals met the fearsome Duke Blue Devils at the Lucas Oil Stadium in Indianapolis. It was sure to be a tough game: Fans consider the historically great Blue Devils to be NCAA "blue bloods," or basketball royalty.

It was Louisville's seventh year in a row making it to the tournament, though it had been a while since they had won it all, way back in 1986. But the 2012–13 Cardinals were unstoppable.

Coach Rick Pitino led the squad, which featured players like senior guard Peyton Siva, junior center Gorgui Dieng, freshman center Montrezl Harrell, and junior guard Russ Smith. All four would later make it to the NBA. Role players like KEVIN WARE, a sophomore from Conyers, Georgia, and the first guard off the bench, were also instrumental in the team's success that season. Ware was a solid defender, but fans would remember him for much more than his steals and blocks at the end of that day's game.

With 6:33 left in the first half, Louisville had a 1-point lead on Duke. Duke's junior guard, Tyler Thornton, had just nailed a three-pointer from the wing. Ware described his attempt to stop Thornton in the seconds that led up to one of the most unforgettable injuries in NCAA tourney history—or in all of sports history:

"I remember bursting up to block the shot, and while I was in the air, turning my head back to watch the ball as it made its way to the basket. I wasn't looking at where I was going to land. I remember my feet hitting the ground. I remember my body hitting the floor. I remember that the first thing I saw was Coach Pitino looking down at me as I was lying on the sideline. He looked like he'd seen a ghost."

Ware had suffered a terrible break to his tibia, or shinbone. The entire arena went deathly silent. Ware seemed to still be in shock—before the tremendous pain kicked in. His teammates even heard him say, "Don't worry about me. I'll be fine." After Ware was rushed to the hospital, the game continued. Louisville forward Chane Behanan wore Ware's jersey for the last few seconds of the game to show respect for his injured teammate. Ware's absence gave Louisville the extra motivation to beat the brakes off Duke 85–63, and the Cardinals went on to defeat the Michigan Wolverines for the national championship.

Once the word got out about the injury, many famous pro players, like LeBron James and the late, great Kobe Bryant, sent out mad love and respect via Twitter and text messages to Ware. Meanwhile, the surgery to fix Ware's leg took more than two hours. Doctors compared his compound fracture to the kind of injury that usually results from bad car accidents or steep falls. They inserted a large titanium rod into his tibia and secured it with screws. They put my man Kev's leg back together again like a LEGO set.

Miraculously, Kevin returned the very next season, but he wasn't fully healed yet and only appeared in nine games. In 2016, he began his professional career in Europe, and has played for several pro teams around the world since. He may be notorious as the kid who broke his leg during the Louisville–Duke game, but two things are for sure: 1) He won't let that incident define him, and 2) There is no quit in Kevin Ware.

PLANET BASKETBALL

HOOPS GO GLOBAL

Basketball may have been invented in Massachusetts way back in the 1890s, but one thing's for sure: The whole world loves to hoop.

For the last few decades, the NBA has been full of incredible international ballers, from dependable role players to Hall of Famers like Hakeem Olajuwon (Nigeria) and Dirk Nowitzki (Germany). Some of the very best current NBA superstars are from outside the United States, like Giannis Antetokounmpo (Greece), Luka Dončić (Slovenia), Joel Embiid (Cameroon), Nikola Jokić (Serbia), Rudy Gobert (France), and Ben Simmons (Australia).

But great American hoopers don't only play in the NBA or WNBA. There are a ton of star players who land in places like Spain, China, Greece, Czechia, and dozens of other countries to fulfill their basketball dreams. A lot of the time that's the only option for great players turning pro, and that's definitely cool, too. Many play overseas before, after, or even during their NBA and WNBA careers.

There are many exciting, beautiful places for ballers to visit around the world, from Asia to Europe to Africa. Overseas players may not make the megabucks that NBA players do, but they can still make a great living in fiercely competitive leagues. Top players in Europe like Nando De Colo, Nick Calathes, and Jan Vesely make a couple million dollars annually. Not bad.

You might not have heard of any of these guys before, but the "ball is life" attitude has spread all over the globe. Make sure to check out some of the best basketball leagues beyond the NBA. Some teams even float between leagues, which you don't see in the United States. Take a squad like Real Madrid, for instance—they are monsters on the court. They've won dozens of championships across various leagues. Now that's ballin'.

TOP TWELVE
INTERNATIONAL
LEAGUES
(IN NO PARTICULAR ORDER)

★ **SPAIN:** Liga ACB, est. 1983

★ **EUROPE:** EuroLeague, est. 2000

★ **TURKEY:** Basketball Super League, est. 1966

★ **CHINA:** Chinese Basketball Association, est. 1995

★ **AUSTRALIA:** National Basketball League, est. 1979

★ **RUSSIA:** VTB United League, est. 2008

★ **GERMANY:** Basketball Bundesliga, est. 1966

★ **ITALY:** Lega Basket Serie A, est. 1920

★ **EUROPE:** ABA League, est. 2001

★ **LITHUANIA:** LKL, est. 1993

★ **AFRICA:** Basketball Africa League, est. 2019

★ **BRAZIL:** Novo Basquete Brasil, est. 2008

CHAPTER 3

RADICAL RECORDS

UNIQUE STATS AND NUMBERS

Minutes. Rebounds. Assists. Double-doubles. Triple-doubles. Championship rings. League MVPs. You name it! If there's one thing that all athletes have in common, it's their drive to put up big numbers, set and break records, and win as many awards as possible. And don't forget about finishing number one when the clock winds down to zero and that buzzer sounds.

Basketball is full of wild stats and numbers. Here are some of the lesser-known or important records by big-time players that you need to hear about.

THE HIGHEST-SCORING GAME EVER

DeVRY HOYAS VS. TROY STATE TROJANS

On January 12, 1992, the Sartain Hall arena in Troy, Alabama, was only half full. The crowd that did show up had no idea they would be witnessing a slugfest for the ages.

The visiting Hoyas of DeVry Institute of Atlanta had only seven available players that day. They were not an official NCAA team, unlike their talented opponents, the NCAA Division II Trojans of Troy State. The Trojans used a "run and gun" offense that was all about pace, movement, and launching as many shots as possible. Coach Don Maestri told his players to move the ball up and down the court as fast as they could, but he didn't place a lot of emphasis

GO! Trojans

HOME 258 20:00 GUEST 141

on defense. After tip-off, it took nearly a minute before the Trojans made the first basket—and then came a tsunami of scoring.

With a hail of three-pointers and a barrage of dunks, Troy State set an NCAA record with 123 points by halftime. They were making baskets every 12.6 seconds! This is how it went for most of the contest: A Trojan player would snatch a defensive rebound and toss it to a teammate at the half-court line, then that player would pass it to another teammate at the three-point line, and before the Hoyas could blink, *BOOM!* Another trey was launched. In that first half of the game, they hit 21 threes. Sick. Even the exhausted referees couldn't keep up with the frenzied tempo.

After halftime, Troy State came out of the locker room with the fire still set on high. Every Trojan bucket for the first 6 minutes and 45 seconds of the second half was either a three-pointer or a dunk. After one measly layup, they went back to hitting shots from downtown or rockin' the rim from inside the paint. When the team reached 200 points, the scoreboard had to be reset back at zero—it didn't go that high!

Troy State's leading scorer was star forward Terry McCord, with 41 points. Backup guard Brian Simpson played only

15 minutes, but he scored 37 points, the second most on the team. He attempted 29 shots, 26 of them from behind the arc. Meanwhile, Dartez Daniel of the Hoyas collected a game-high 42 points, but it wasn't enough. Four Trojans hit 29 points, and ten out of the eleven guys who got some clock scored double digits.

The final score? Troy State 258, DeVry 141. What?!? That's 399 points total, an NCAA record that still stands—and probably will forever.

Troy State even broke the record they'd set in the first part of the game: most points scored in a half with 123, adding a whopping 135 in the second half. Other untouchable records set during this game were most three-pointers attempted and made by a team (51 out of 109), most attempted and successful shots (102 out of 190), most assists by one team (65), and most total offensive and defensive boards (94).

The next season, Troy State moved up a class and played in Division I, while the Hoyas of DeVry disbanded their basketball program. I might shut mine down, too, after a game like that. But, hey, give respect where it's due: 141 points is plenty impressive, too!

LONG
SHOTS

THE FARTHEST BASKETS EVER MADE

Okay, just so we're clear, we're talking about the longest shots made during an official game, at both the college and NBA levels. Sure, crazy trick shots by YouTubers like Dude Perfect are no doubt mind-boggling. Making a basket by dropping a ball from the Empire State Building while blindfolded and balancing a vase on your nose is cool, too, but what about when it counts? Like when that clock is ticking, and you need to hit a buzzer-beater to win the game?

In the history of college basketball, the longest shot ever made was 89 feet, 10 inches. (On a 94-foot court, that's almost the entire length of the floor!) On February 7, 1985, in a game

between the Thundering Herd of Marshall University and the Mountaineers of Appalachian State University, Marshall senior point guard BRUCE MORRIS was in the right place at the right time. I mean, there was most definitely a little bit of talent involved, but a smidgen of luck, too. A big ol' smidgen.

A Marshall player blocked a shot by Appalachian State, and the rock fell toward the baseline and right into Morris's mitts. With less than 3 seconds left on the clock for the half, Morris cocked his arm back like a quarterback and heaved that ball. The shot had no arc at all. It was practically a fastball, a beaming blur of orange all the way down toward the other goal. The line-drive shot sank perfectly through the net right at the buzzer and the crowd at the Cam Henderson Center in Huntington, West Virginia, went bananas. Did this guy just make a basket spanning the *entire* length of the court? What?! Morris himself said, "I probably couldn't hit the backboard from there in a million tries." Today, you can find his footprints painted on the Cam Henderson floor, right in the spot where he took his magical shot.

In the NBA, the longest shot ever made during a game came courtesy of Charlotte Hornets point guard BARON DAVIS on February 17, 2001. My man asked for the rock in the third quarter with only 0.7 seconds left—now that's swagger. The confident Baron took a simple inbound pass and launched the ball with all his might. With just a touch of arc, the ball sailed right in. The really cool thing about Baron's feat was that he called it would go in as he threw it. The shot measured exactly 89 feet and broke a record that had stood for twenty-four years, ever since Chicago Bulls guard Norm Van Lier hit an 84-foot launch on January 19, 1977, against the San Antonio Spurs.

A lot of players have come close, attempting half-court and almost full-court buckets at all levels of play. LeBron James made an 83-footer in 2007, and Indiana Pacers center Herb Williams banked one from 81 feet in 1986. In the WNBA in 1999, Houston Comets All-Star guard TERESA WEATHERSPOON made a legendary Finals game winner from beyond half-court as time expired—it's now called simply "The Shot." But to be honest with you, skill has little to do with making a full-court lob. Sure, you've gotta be strong enough to launch it that far. But unless you're like Stephen Curry and you actually *practice* hitting court-length shots, it's mostly luck, a dash of adrenaline, and a little more luck.

And speaking of Steph . . .

THE THREE-POINT KING

STEPHEN CURRY LEADS THE PACK

Three-pointers are so common in today's game that hoops fans sometimes forget that the long-ball didn't always exist. The American Basketball League (ABL) was the first pro league to add a three-point line back in 1961, but the NBA wouldn't include the exciting long-range shot until 1979. College basketball added that magic three-point line in 1986, and high school was last, making it official nationwide in 1987.

Make no mistake, players have been shooting long-range jump shots since the game's inception. It's a definite craft—you can't just roll out of bed and fire off an ugly shot with awkward form. The guys who have etched themselves into the record books as the best sharpshooters in the game have practiced thousands of three-pointers since they were kids. But who is *the* guy, the all-time three-point champion?

For many years, basketball fans used to think of just a few names: Hall of Famer and Indiana Pacers legend REGGIE MILLER; former shooting guard and current Golden State Warriors head coach STEVE KERR; and two-time NBA Champ, ten-time All-Star, and Olympic gold medalist RAY ALLEN. But since 2021, the reigning king of three-point-land is Wardell Stephen Curry II—you probably know him as Steph. That's right: Golden State Warriors All-Galaxy point guard and team captain STEPHEN CURRY.

With his long-range shooting prowess, Steph has helped change the way the greatest basketball minds view the game. Today's sport is much more reliant on three-pointers, and many more big men are expected to shoot beyond the arc. (This is called "stretching the floor"—and it's much harder for defenses when anyone can shoot from anywhere!) With the huge success of the Warriors, it's easy to see Steph's league-wide influence, along with his fellow sharpshooting "Splash Brother," the great Klay Thompson.

What sets Steph apart from the legion of so many legendary shooters in NBA history is distance and accuracy. Steph will pull up from anywhere on the court, which makes him extremely hard to defend. He'll practically shoot from the parking lot. He is the most accurate three-point shooter who has attempted at least 1,700 shots, making 43 percent of them. (Steve Kerr, at 45 percent accuracy, only took 1,599 shots from beyond the arc.) Plus, Curry has amassed his threes in a shorter amount of time, with fewer attempts than any other all-time player. He also owns the record for draining the most three-point shots in a single season, with 402.

Before Steph, Hall of Famer Ray Allen broke the record for the most threes in 2011 when he swiped it from Reggie Miller, who had held the all-time mark for thirteen years. The record at that point was 2,560. Allen, who is also famous for playing high school baller Jesus Shuttlesworth in the movie *He Got Game*, held the record for eleven years and ended his career with 2,973 threes. It took him 1,300 games to eclipse Reggie . . . but it took Steph only 789 games to snatch the top spot.

GREATEST HOOPS MOVIES

Here are some other unforgettable basketball flicks. How many of these have you seen already?

★ **LIKE MIKE** `2002` starring Bow Wow

★ **SPACE JAM** `1996` starring Michael Jordan

★ **SPACE JAM: A NEW LEGACY** `2021` starring LeBron James

★ **HOOSIERS** `1986` starring Gene Hackman

★ **AIR BUD** `1998` starring a golden retriever named Air Buddy

★ **TEEN WOLF** `1985` starring Michael J. Fox

★ **CORNBREAD, EARL AND ME** `1975` starring Laurence Fishburne

★ **LOVE & BASKETBALL** `2000` starring Sanaa Lathan and Omar Epps

★ **HOOP DREAMS** `1994` starring William Gates and Arthur Agee

★ **COACH CARTER** `2005` starring Samuel L. Jackson

On December 14, 2021, in a game against the New York Knicks in the hallowed Madison Square Garden, Steph became the new career leader in three-point shots made in the NBA. Both Mr. Miller and Mr. Allen were sitting in the stands to bear witness. When Curry broke the record in the first quarter, reaching 2,974, the game was halted so that the entire arena could cheer on that mind-boggling accomplishment.

And who was the person Steph gave the ball to? His pops, of course, Charlotte Hornets legend Dell Curry. Steph saluted the crowd, who were all on their feet. He celebrated with teammates, and then embraced and gave respect to Miller and Allen. They even took a few pics together—just an awesome scene. But you know what's even more awesome, and even more mind-boggling? It's entirely possible that no one might ever catch him. He now has more than 3,000 and counting!

WHO'S GONNA STOP US?!

THE LONGEST WINNING STREAKS

Winning streaks are a funny phenomenon. And not just in sports: Sometimes you find yourself going for days, weeks, and even months without losing at something. Maybe it's getting all A's in a particular class, or beating your friends to the bus stop in the morning. It could even be something as small as defeating your younger cousin in *NBA 2K* for the 237th time. (C'mon, give her a chance to win at least one!) But no matter what it is, winning consecutively is a mindset. You start feeling like you can do no wrong. Like you're *supposed* to win. And it can be contagious.

In basketball, like any other team sport, it's amazing how an entire group of people, from the coaching staff all the way down to the guy sitting on the edge of the bench, can get bitten by the winning bug. And sometimes, it feels like there will be no end to the victories. Let's look at a few of basketball's greatest winning streaks.

First up, the **1971-72 LOS ANGELES LAKERS** set an astounding NBA record for the most consecutive victories. The streak began on November 5, 1971, with a 110–106 win over the Baltimore Bullets (today's Washington Wizards). They didn't lose until two months later, on January 9, 1972, with a score of 120–104 against Kareem Abdul-Jabbar's Milwaukee Bucks. At the streak's end, the Lakers had amassed 33 straight wins. The only team to come close were the Golden State Warriors, with 28 wins over two seasons from 2014 to 2016.

Those '72 Lakers, led by Hall of Fame coach Bill Sharman, were unbelievable. They went on to finish the season with a bonkers record of 69-13. That win-loss record stood for twenty-four years, when some guy named Michael Jordan and his 1995–96 Chicago Bulls put up a 72-10. (Show-offs.) But the

'72 Lakers crew were a bunch of All-Stars and golden boys. The team featured five Hall of Famers: Elgin Baylor (eleven-time All-Star), Gail Goodrich (five-time All-Star), Jerry West (yep, the guy in the NBA logo), Pat Riley (a future all-time great head coach), and Wilt Chamberlain (Mr. 100-point game). The NBA named the '72 Lakers as one of the ten greatest NBA teams of all time during the league's fiftieth anniversary ceremony in 1996.

Meanwhile, in men's college hoops, the **UCLA BRUINS** hold the record for longest winning streak. John Wooden, arguably the greatest college basketball coach of all time, led the Bruins through almost four seasons without a loss. From January 30, 1971, to January 19, 1974, the Bruins won 88 straight games with the help of this sensei of basketball. But if you think that's special, check out the women's team at UConn. Led by Hall of Famer Geno Auriemma, who has coached the **UCONN HUSKIES** to eleven NCAA championships since 1985, the team went on a four-year-long regular season streak. Beginning with a win against Creighton on November 23, 2014, and ending with a crushing loss to the Lady Bears of Baylor on January 3, 2019, the Huskies won 126 regular season games. That's four whole seasons!

But, like I told you, it all comes to an end eventually. Your little cousin will rise up and crush you on *NBA 2K* someday—and I hope she records it.

THE QUADRUPLE- AND QUINTUPLE-DOUBLE CLUB

BIG-TIME DOUBLE-DIGIT STATS

A player achieves a double-double if they get double-digit stats in two of these five categories: points, rebounds, assists, blocks, and steals. If the same player racks up double-digit stats in three of those categories, it's called a triple-double. How about four? Quadruple-double. But the "Sasquatch" of stats accomplishments is the super-elusive *quintuple*-double.

The NBA didn't begin counting steals and blocks until the 1973–74 season, so it's possible that some players might have achieved the quintuple before then, including the almighty WILT CHAMBERLAIN. He's the only player to record eight 40–40 double-doubles, which is when you collect 40 points and 40 rebounds in a single game!

Hall of Famer and Spurs great **TIM DUNCAN** holds the record for the most double-doubles with 841. The hoopers on top of the triple-doubles hill are All-Star point guard **RUSSELL WESTBROOK**, with more than 190 and counting, followed by Oscar Robertson ("The Big O"), with 181. They are the only players in the league's history to average a triple-double for an entire season. From 2016 to 2019, Westbrook had three consecutive seasons averaging a triple-double every game, and the most in a single season (42). Incredible.

Quadruple-doubles are more rare. It takes a different caliber of baller, and only four NBA players have ever pulled it off:

★ **NATE THURMOND** of the Chicago Bulls was the first person to ever log a quadruple-double (22 points, 12 blocks, 14 rebounds, 13 assists on October 18, 1974). "Nate the Great," a Hall of Famer, is considered one of the greatest defensive players ever.

★ San Antonio Spurs shooting guard **ALVIN ROBERTSON** inked his name in the history books on February 18, 1986, by hitting 20 buckets, snatching 11 boards, dishing 10 assists, and stealing the rock from the Phoenix Suns 10 times.

★ Houston Rockets icon and Hall of Famer HAKEEM "THE DREAM" OLAJUWON did it on March 29, 1990, against the Bucks. He racked up 18 points, 10 assists, 11 blocks, and 16 rebounds.

★ The most recent NBA quadruple-double happened on February 17, 1994. Hall of Fame center DAVID "THE ADMIRAL" ROBINSON of the San Antonio Spurs recorded 34 points, 10 rebounds, 10 blocks, and 10 assists against the Pistons.

And now, for the quintuple-doubles: The most shocking thing is that they were high school kids. The most recent was center AIMEE OERTNER of Northern Lehigh High School in Slatington, Pennsylvania. She showed out in a game on January 7, 2012, with 26 points, 20 rebounds, 10 assists, 10 steals, and 11 blocks.

During her senior year in 2007, forward ALEX MONTGOMERY did it for Lincoln High School in Tacoma, Washington. Alex went on to play at Georgia Tech and then joined the New York Liberty as the tenth overall pick of the 2011 WNBA draft. She also hooped with the San Antonio Stars and the Chicago Sky of the WNBA.

But the very first person to attach a quintuple-double to their name was WNBA legend and four-time Olympic gold medalist TAMIKA CATCHINGS. As a student at Duncanville High in Texas in 1997, she scored 25 points, grabbed 10 steals, blocked 10 shots, dished 11 assists, and collected 18 rebounds on the way to making history.

NOTHING *BUT* RELIABLE NET

THE MOST CONSECUTIVE FREE THROWS EVER MADE

When you see a player about to fire a free throw shot, you may not be able to tell right away how good a shooter they are. Maybe they're one of those kids who spent hours working on their technique in middle school—but the big-game pressure makes them miss. One thing's for sure: Free throws are a *huuuuge* key to winning the game. And if you're the one standing at the free throw line with the team and the fans depending on you? The most important thing you can do is stay as cool as the other side of the pillow.

It doesn't matter how many distracting signs the crowd is holding up behind the backboard. People are counting on you to

hit the bottom of that net with the game on the line. Some players are so dependable when they shoot from the "charity stripe" that you'd be willing to bet a dollar (or maybe even a little more) that they'll sink it.

So who are those free throw sharpshooters and all-timers? **KARL "THE MAILMAN" MALONE** made the most free throw shots ever, with 9,787 over the course of his nineteen-season Hall of Fame career, almost entirely with the Utah Jazz. But he hit only 74.2 percent of them. Just three players in NBA history have scored more than 90 percent of their shots: point guards Steph Curry (.9087), Steve Nash (.9043), and Mark Price (.9039). And which player hit the most consecutive shots in a row? Can you imagine hitting free throws for so long that you could probably wear a blindfold and still knock them down?

Ever heard of **MICHEAL WILLIAMS**? I know, it's a pretty common-sounding name. You might have a Michael Williams in one of your classes. But this Mike had creative parents who switched around the "a" and the "e" in his first name. *Micheal* Williams played for six NBA teams in eleven seasons. Check this out: Over eight long months, Micheal was Mr. Automatic at the free throw line for the Minnesota Timberwolves. Between March 24 and November 9, 1993, he made 97 straight free throws in a row. Sick!

But the all-time amateur record for consecutive free throws is in a stratosphere all its own. It belongs to a dairy farmer from California named **TED ST. MARTIN**. A high school basketball player in Naches, Washington, Ted had never been a star on the team. But after hitting baskets over and over (and over and over) on an old hoop that he had nailed to the side of his barn, he gained the confidence to take down the Guinness World Record.

After hours and hours of practice on the farm, sixty-one-year-old Ted St. Martin was making hundreds of straight buckets and knew he could easily demolish the record. So he hit 200 straight free throws, no sweat. But he wasn't done yet. Ted loved shooting hoops so much that he kept breaking the record, sometimes even his own, over a twenty-two-year span. His last recorded number was 5,221 straight on April 28, 1996! It took him only seven hours to do it. "Only"? It would probably have taken me seven lifetimes!

1,333 W'S

THE MOST COACHING WINS IN BOYS' HIGH SCHOOL HISTORY

Some say the greatest coach in NBA history was Red Auerbach. In his career, he won 938 regular-season games and an astounding nine NBA titles in 17 seasons with the Boston Celtics. Some think the best college coach of all time might be UCLA's John Wooden, who won ten NCAA championships during his twenty-nine-year career. These legends sure racked up a *ton* of W's, but did you know that the winningest boys' high school coach has more wins than either of them?

ROBERT HUGHES was born in Oklahoma, but he made a pretty good name for himself in the state of Texas. Coach Hughes played college ball at Texas Southern University, a historically Black college, from 1951 to 1954. As a forward and guard during his senior campaign, he won TSU's Athlete of the Year. It was at TSU that Hughes learned a fast-paced style of play from Coach Edward Adams.

Hughes was eventually drafted by the Boston Celtics in 1954, but because of an injury, he decided to call it quits as a player. Hughes's old mentor Adams nudged him into coaching. He helped him get hired at a high school in Fort Worth, Texas, in 1958, during the height of segregation in the south. It was a tall task: I. M. Terrell High had been suffering a losing streak for twenty years. But the young coach soon had those kids running and gunning.

Coach Hughes trained his players like track or marathon athletes. He pushed them to go at a nonstop pace without running out of gas, so that the opposing team would wave the white flag from sheer exhaustion. One of his mottos was "Don't Get Outworked!"

Coach Hughes was also a serious disciplinarian who demanded the best out of his kids, both on and off the court.

He made a name for himself city- and statewide, even though segregation was still in effect. He and his players faced racism from White referees, opponents, and fans when they traveled to play at other schools. Sometimes they were barred from entering certain restaurants and lodges, and the all-White teams refused to play them. But none of that stopped Mr. Hughes from piling on wins.

When Terrell High closed in 1973, Coach Hughes had collected 373 wins and three Prairie View Interscholastic League championships. He then went across town to Dunbar High School, where everyone called him "The Sultan of Stop Six," named after the predominantly Black neighborhood in southeast Fort Worth, where Dunbar is located. Hughes stayed there until his retirement in 2005, at the age of seventy-seven, after a three-decade stint of running other teams off the court.

Overall, he stockpiled an astronomical 1,333 wins, notched 35 district and five state championships, and helped send hundreds of young Black men to college. He coached for forty-seven years and left just as strong an impression on the city of Fort Worth and Dunbar High as Coach Auerbach did for the Celtics or Coach Wooden did for UCLA. Coach Robert Hughes, also known as "The Duke of Dunbar," was inducted into the Basketball Hall of Fame on March 31, 2017.

MAN OF IRON

1,192 CONSECUTIVE GAMES PLAYED

A lot of people think that Tony Stark is the only Iron Man out there. Nope. Basketball's own Iron Man is **A.C. GREEN**, who hooped in 1,192 consecutive regular-season games. Not even Tony Stark could pull off that feat.

In 1985, the Los Angeles Lakers drafted A.C. Green out of Oregon State as the twenty-third pick of the first round. To enter the NBA is exciting enough, but joining an incredible Lakers team the season after they had won a championship would be a life-altering experience for any young athlete. The team was electric. They were the talk of the sports world, and fans called them the "Showtime Lakers." This flamboyant squad,

led by Hall of Famers Magic Johnson, Kareem Abdul-Jabbar, and James Worthy, was like a band of rock stars living it up in Hollywood. But the staunchly religious young man from Oregon did not let the lures of the big city alter his beliefs or work ethic.

The sight of both his parents working hard every single day, regardless of illness or anything else that would keep them from earning a living and raising their family, stayed with A.C. forever. After a thumb injury kept him out for three games in his second season, the power forward never missed another game. (You might have missed three days of school in just one year!) A.C. became an instant starter with "Showtime" and would go on to play pro ball for the next sixteen years. He even won three championships with the Lakers in 1987, 1988, and 2000.

November 19, 1986, marked the beginning of his record-breaking streak of 832 starts and 36,552 minutes. He never sat out, even after he left the Lakers in 1993 to play for the Phoenix Suns, the Dallas

Mavericks, and then back with the Lakers for a season in 2000. In all that time, he never let his teammates or his fans down. Can you imagine playing fourteen straight years of pro b-ball and not missing a single game? He played during three decades, sporting his famous Jheri curl hairstyle and sometimes even a full face mask to help him grind through a record-breaking 1,192 straight games.

Green definitely got banged up plenty throughout his career, but nothing was serious enough to keep him from lacing up his sneakers and ballin'. Once, in 1996, an opponent from the New York Knicks named J. R. Reid purposefully hit him with a powerful forearm, knocking out two of A.C.'s teeth. They just flew out of his mouth and slid across the hardwood floor like a pair of dice. But do you think that stopped A.C.? Of course not. He just scooped up those teeth and came back to play in the very next game, keeping the streak alive. He leaned on his religious beliefs to give him strength to stay in the game.

Major salute to Mr. Green for sticking to his convictions and not allowing the distractions of being a big-time athlete compromise his beliefs and dedication to the grind.

THE SELFLESS SCOTT SKILES

THE RECORD FOR THE MOST ASSISTS IN A GAME

Whether you call them "dimes" or "dishes," assists are essential to any team's success in hoops. Ever heard a basketball coach holler, "Find the open player!"? That's one of the main tasks for a point guard: to see the entire court and maximize the talents of everyone around them. Every winning team needs a leader who practices that selflessness so their teammates can shine. Because when we all shine, we win.

An NBA point guard named **SCOTT SKILES** understood that well, first during his high school days as an Indiana state champion with the Plymouth High Pilgrims, and then as a star point guard for the Michigan State Spartans. The Milwaukee Bucks chose him as the twenty-second pick of the 1986 draft, and then soon traded him to the Indiana Pacers, where he played only two seasons. But in 1989, he was picked in an expansion draft to play for a brand-new team called the Orlando Magic. It was there that the wizardry began.

Skiles was a benchwarmer for his first four years in the NBA. Then, in 1990, Skiles's fifth year as a pro, Orlando named him their starting point guard and his game finally began to heat up. All of his stats immediately got a boost, but his assist totals skyrocketed.

As the "quarterback" of a basketball team's offense, it is essential that the point guard gets the ball into the hands of their scorers. Of course, if you're an accurate shooter, you create open shots for yourself, too. (Think of masters like Steph Curry, Ja Morant, or Trae Young.) Skiles could do both. He was a scrappy, hardworking little guard, and no single game exhibited his grit and leadership more than the one on December 30, 1990: the day that Skiles and his 6-23 Magic played the equally miserable 6-22 Denver Nuggets at the Orlando Arena.

Denver's freewheeling, fast-break offense favored Orlando that night. Skiles figured that if his opponents were going to play superfast and dish the ball around, he'd do the same thing for his crew.

Skiles played 44 minutes that game, more than any other player. He was the third-leading scorer on the team with 22 points, but that wasn't the story. He went assist-crazy and passed to whoever was open. Four backup players and four starters scored in double figures. (I think he could have found his mom for an open three from the bleachers!) By the end of the night, Skiles had collected a massive 30 assists. He had bested the previous single-game assists record of 29, set in 1978 by New Jersey Nets guard Kevin Porter. Thanks to the little 6'1" general from Plymouth, Indiana, the Magic went on to win the game 155–116.

Skiles's record still holds strong today, more than thirty years later. Shout-out to all the Scott Skiles–like players of the world who understand that it's not always about you. It's also about how much you influence, encourage, and create magic for the people around you.

CHAPTER 4

TRIUMPHANT TURNAROUNDS

CLASSIC COMEBACKS BY TEAMS AND PLAYERS

Basketball requires strategy and skill to win. Of course, you need a squad of sharpshooting assassins, tenacious defenders, and high-flying dunk artists. But you also gotta have heart. You need the fire to stage an incredible comeback, even when the other team has a double-digit lead with the clock winding down and a win seems impossible. Or even when doctors and fans say you'll never make it back to the court after a tough injury or illness.

Those kinds of victories take a rare type of player: a true leader, a brave and fearless baller with ice water running through their veins. No ordinary player or team could muster up the intestinal fortitude to climb back out of a hole and leave the opposing team's fanbase dragging along the ground and sloshing in their own salty tears. So, here's the lesson: Never. Count. Anyone. Out.

DRAGONS BREATHE FIRE

THE LARGEST COMEBACK IN NCAA MEN'S TOURNAMENT HISTORY

At halftime, the DELAWARE FIGHTIN' BLUE HENS squad was feeling great. They were on the road, playing at the Daskalakis Athletic Center right in the heart of Philly, the home of the DREXEL DRAGONS. As the first-half clock ticked down, they were just burning the wings right off the Dragons. With 2:36 before halftime, the scoreboard read: Delaware 53, Drexel 19. A 34-point lead?! It was a wrap. Done. Drexel had already lost to Delaware 72–66 earlier in this 2018 season. And now it looked as if the Blue Hens were going to sweep the Dragons.

Making matters worse, Drexel entered the game following a four-game losing streak. Their only sliver of hope was the fact that both teams had the same record: 12-18. After all, they weren't being outmuscled by a powerhouse program like Kentucky, Kansas, or UNC. But they knew they needed to come out of that locker room and play like a different team for the second half. Drexel's head coach, Zach Spiker, told his crew to

GREATEST BUZZER-BEATERS EVER

★ **MARCH 28, 1992:** DUKE BEAT KENTUCKY 104–103 IN THE NCAA MEN'S TOURNAMENT

Grant Hill of Duke threw a full-court, bull's-eye pass to Christian Laettner, who hit a turnaround bucket at the free throw line. Classic clutch move.

★ **MAY 7, 1989:** BULLS BEAT CAVALIERS 101–100 IN THE PLAYOFFS

The king of all NBA buzzer-beaters is "His Airness," Michael Jordan, who had nine in his career. His first and most famous was a last-second jumper from just beyond the free throw line, called simply "The Shot."

★ **MAY 13, 2004:** LAKERS BEAT SPURS 74–73 IN THE PLAYOFFS

Point guard Derek Fisher sank his classic jump shot buzzer-beater with only 0.4 seconds left on the clock.

tighten up and be more aggressive. Losing four games in a row can affect a team's collective confidence. But these hoopers were tired of losing, and a historic comeback was brewing.

Drexel's plan of action was to increase the pace of the game and force Delaware to make mistakes and take risky shots.

★ APRIL 3, 1994: NORTH CAROLINA BEATS LOUISIANA TECH 60–59 IN THE NCAA WOMEN'S TOURNAMENT

Charlotte Smith of UNC came up clutch and hit a three with only 0.7 seconds on the clock to win the first national championship in Tar Heels women's basketball history.

★ MAY 12, 2019: RAPTORS BEAT 76ERS 92–90 IN THE PLAYOFFS

Kawhi Leonard hit a clutch corner jumper, which left his hands at the 0.5-second mark. It bounced on the rim three times and dramatically fell through the net. The crowd went bananas and the Raptors went on to win their first championship.

★ DECEMBER 15, 2021: PELICANS BEAT THUNDER 113–110

Point guard Devonte' Graham hit the longest game-winner in NBA history, sinking a 61 footer from the other team's three-point line!

And when the Blue Hens missed, the Dragons' job was to snatch those loose boards and convert them into points. That's just what they did. (Drexel grabbed 36 total rebounds, 7 more than Delaware, and 25 of them were defensive.) The Dragons began the second half with a big 18–4 run. Delaware's biggest lead in the second half was 16 points, but Drexel kept chipping away at it.

That's when the Delaware players started getting nervous and Drexel players started getting confident. Maybe, just maybe, they could walk out of that arena with a victory. Their star point guard, a transfer from the University of Missouri named Tramaine Isabell, scored 29 points, the most by any player in the game. Thirty-eight of the points scored after the half were either the result of a shot he hit, or one he assisted in making.

With 10 seconds left in the game, the teams were tied at 83 points apiece. Drexel had the rock, and who do you think took the shot? Isabell, of course. He went for a trey with 2 seconds left in the game but was fouled, and then he sank two of three foul shots to win it.

Final score: Drexel 85, Delaware 83. The Dragons had clawed their way back from a 34-point deficit. Outstanding!

The largest comeback in Division I basketball history prior to this game was in 1950, when Duke found a way to climb out of their 32-point hole and beat Tulane 74–72. Almost seventy years later, the Drexel Dragons made history with a game that was the highlight of their season. Their final record for the 2017–18 season was a meager 13–20. But they were forever cemented in the record books for the gutsiest, most unexpected comeback in NCAA history.

THE "MIRACLE MINUTE"

COLLEGE RIVALS DUKE IT OUT

The **MARYLAND TERRAPINS** and **DUKE BLUE DEVILS** are serious rivals. Think Celtics–Lakers, only at the collegiate level. The teams haven't played since Maryland left the Atlantic Coast Conference (ACC) for the Big 10 Conference in 2014. But for a long time the rivals squared off all the time, and Maryland mostly just nipped at the ankles of "big dog" Duke University.

After 177 games between the rivals, Duke is firmly on top with a strong 114-63 record. And in one of those legendary matchups, on January 27, 2001, Maryland scared the giblets out of Duke fans. Sometimes you think the game is won—and then the tables can turn in less than 60 seconds.

That night, Duke's victory run of 22 straight road wins looked like it was coming to an end in Maryland. They were 18-1 that season and undefeated in the conference. For most of this game, Maryland had a comfortable lead. By the time there were only 65 seconds left, Duke had closed the gap a little but still trailed by 12 points. The Maryland fans were loud and in pre-celebration mode. Some chanted "OVERRATED!" (*Clap, clap, clap-clap-clap.*) "OVERRATED!" (*Clap, clap, clap-clap-clap.*) But the Terrapins left enough time on the clock, and the Blue Devils somehow remembered they were top dogs.

First, Duke guard Nate James sunk a three-pointer. Then Maryland hit one of two foul shots. 90–80. Then Duke superstar guard Jason Williams made a layup. After just a moment of play, Duke stole the ball from Maryland's shooting guard Drew Nicholas, and Williams got it back to knock down a three. All of that happened within 6 seconds! 90–85.

There were now 48 seconds left and Terrapin fans started biting their nails. No more "overrated" chants. Meanwhile, the Duke players had morphed into a pack of hyenas. Nicholas went to the foul line and missed both of his shots. Duke got the board, and Jason Williams (who else?) tossed up another jumper from three-point land. Just like that, Duke was within 2 points, 90–88.

With 30 seconds left, Maryland had the ball, but Duke snatched a weak inbound pass as the clock continued to tick. They frantically passed around the rock until it landed in the hands of their three-point specialist and scoring machine, forward Mike Dunleavy Jr. He missed a shot that would have given the Blue Devils the lead, but Nate James grabbed the clutch offensive rebound. He tried to tip it in as well but was hacked by a couple of Terrapins. James went to the foul line and hit both attempts—cold as ice! Tie game, 90–90.

Jason Williams brought Duke back to life within that "Miracle Minute," as it came to be known. But overtime belonged to senior forward and team captain Shane Battier, a future NBA champion. He went down as one of the greatest defensive players in Duke history, and that OT period showed why. Battier made a key block, a steal, and threw in 6 points to help finish off Maryland, 98–96. Don't ever count out a fearsome team like Duke!

HARD TO KEEP A GOOD KING DOWN

A KNICKS LEGEND'S UNBELIEVABLE RETURN

Waaaaay back in the day, in the 1980s (you know, ancient history), most serious knee injuries spelled the end for a pro athlete's career. Nowadays, though, new surgical devices and rehabilitation techniques (aka physical therapy) have made a world of difference. Arthroscopic surgery, for instance, only requires cutting a small incision to fit a little camera that can go inside the knee, believe it or not. A torn meniscus or ACL (anterior cruciate ligament) or patellar tendonitis ("jumper's knee") is no longer a career-ender. But back in 1985, Knicks fans were convinced their hometown star would never play the same way again after suffering a knee injury.

BERNARD KING, a Brooklyn, New York, native and University of Tennessee small forward, was a star from the jump. He was the seventh overall pick by the New Jersey Nets in the 1977 NBA draft, and in his rookie season, King averaged 24.2 points and 9.5 rebounds. But over the next five seasons, he shuffled among three different teams. He was an enigma.

On the court, King was extremely talented, aggressive, and competitive on the hardwood. He was a scoring threat no matter whom he faced. But he got in some trouble off the court and made some bad life decisions. The forward bounced around teams for a while, going from the Nets to the Utah Jazz to the Golden State Warriors, who traded him in 1982 to the New York Knicks. It was back in his hometown of NYC that he became one of the top five players in the league.

ACL

King was a superstar to the faithful crowds at Madison Square Garden and led the league in scoring for the 1984–85 season with an incredible 32.9 points per game. In his magical run with the Knicks, he was also a two-time selection to the All-NBA First Team. But on March 23, 1985, King went up to block a dunk from one of Kansas City's guards, Reggie Theus, and landed awkwardly. The fall broke his right leg, tore cartilage, and shredded his ACL. Knicks fans thought their star's career was finished.

King underwent total reconstructive knee surgery and sat out the entire 1985–86 season. Doctors told him he'd never play in the NBA ever again. But Bernard knew he had the pure will to overcome this setback and one day get back on the court. He trained with a physical therapist for five hours per day for two years straight. That's dedication! He even had a sign on his bedroom wall that read "I WILL NOT BE DENIED."

King finally made his triumphant return to the Knicks on April 10, 1987, against the Milwaukee Bucks. The crowd at Madison Square Garden gave him a standing ovation that seemed to last forever. King only got to play in the final six games of the 1986–87 campaign, missing nearly two full seasons. He averaged 22.7 points per game, but the Knicks soon traded him away to the Washington Bullets, where he would ball for the next four seasons.

King wasn't as explosive as he once was, but he was still a force. Between the ages of thirty-one and thirty-four, he averaged 22.0 points and 4.7 rebounds per game. Not bad at all. In the 1990–91 season he made the All-Star team for the fourth and final time. He retired in 1993 and was inducted into the Basketball Hall of Fame in 2013. In his speech, he credited hard work and support by loved ones and friends for his success.

BIG FIRST-ROUND EXIT

THE FIRST-EVER EIGHT-SEED TO TOPPLE A ONE-SEED

You want to talk about squads? In the 1990s, the **SEATTLE SUPERSONICS** (today's Oklahoma City Thunder) had some serious ballers who made them consistently one of the best in the West. The Chicago Bulls were the top team of the 1990s, but from 1992 to 1998, the "Sonic Boom" played a style of dominant, exciting ball that no one had ever seen before.

In that span, Seattle's record was 357-135 and they won the Pacific Division four times. Spearheading the Sonics was Gary "The Glove" Payton, one of the best point guards in the game at the time, as well as power forward Shawn Kemp, who could

144

jump over the moon. Kemp, known as "The Reign Man," was the league's most freakishly athletic forward who no defense had an answer for. The Sonics were great during the regular season, but there was just one problem: They couldn't keep the party going for the playoffs.

The 1993–94 season was supposed to be the year the Sonics brought home the gold. They had the best record in basketball at 63-19, and they were the number-one seed (of eight total) in the Western Conference playoffs. Their first-round opponents, the 42-40 DENVER NUGGETS, had barely made it into the playoffs. Besides, an eight-seed had never beaten a one-seed before. (Never say "never," right?)

Denver's leader, a third-year defensive dynamo named Dikembe Mutombo, played center like a human flyswatter. The Congolese big man accumulated 336 blocks for that season alone—that's 4.1 per game! Dikembe had brought a scrappy crew with him to battle the Goliath that was Seattle. Point guard Mahmoud Abdul-Rauf, forward LaPhonso Ellis, guard Robert Pack, and veteran forward Reggie Williams had nothing to lose. They fought with everything they had.

The teams played their first two games at the Center Coliseum in Seattle. The Nuggets made a good effort, but they lost both games, 82–106 and 87–97, respectively. Just like that, they were down 0-2 in a best-of-five series that looked to be over already. But the next two games were back home in Denver at the McNichols Sports Arena, and the home-court advantage paid off. The Nuggets finally figured a few things out: The Sonics played a fast-paced game, but if their jumpers didn't fall, if they didn't grab their own boards, and, most of all, if they couldn't fire off uncontested shots, they'd find it hard to win.

Denver won the next two games through defense alone, 110–93 and then 94–85 in overtime. The series was now tied, and the teams headed back to Seattle for the final game. But it didn't matter where they played it: Denver stuck to the same formula and pulled off a shocking 98–94 victory in another epic overtime battle. Dikembe Mutombo had 31 blocks in the series (a record that still stands), and his finger-wagging gesture after a swat became his trademark. He averaged 12.2 rebounds and 6.2 blocks per game.

The moral of this underdog story? It doesn't matter where you are ranked in the beginning. Take it one game at a time and do what you do best.

CINDERELLA MEETS *HER* MATCH

THE LARGEST COMEBACK IN WOMEN'S NCAA TOURNAMENT HISTORY

In the men's and women's NCAA tournaments over the years, Ivy League squads have often played the role of "Cinderella." Those are the under-the-radar teams that unexpectedly spoil the plans of a perennial favorite. Ivy League schools like the University of Pennsylvania (Penn) are known far more for academics than athletics—of course, that doesn't mean their scholar-athletes can't ball with the best of them. But in this epic comeback, even "Cinderella" couldn't quite finish the job.

On March 18, 2017, the twelve-seed PENN QUAKERS team looked as if they were about to eliminate the favored five-seed TEXAS A&M AGGIES in the first round of the 2017 women's tournament.

149

Penn had won thirteen of their last fourteen games and were on a roll. For the first half of the game, it was all Quakers. With 8:59 left in the second half, they led 58–37. A 21-point lead!

The Quakers hit over 50 percent of their shots for the first 30 minutes of the game. They had full control. But for those last 9 minutes or so, Coach Gary Blair of the Aggies decided to try a full-court press to thwart the Penn players. The Quakers were just too comfortable on offense, making basket after basket. But the added pressure caused them to panic.

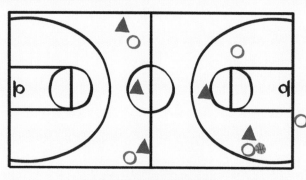

THE FULL-COURT PRESS

Penn missed the last ten shots they attempted in the game, and they turned the ball over seven times within those final 9 minutes. Texas A&M out-rebounded the opposition 16 to 6 in the fourth quarter, getting their brainy Ivy League heads spinning. The Quakers committed nine fouls, which allowed the Aggies to drop thirteen buckets at the foul line. Twenty of their 63 total points came from the "charity stripe." (Hey, it's not as flashy, but free throws win games.) That 21-point deficit shrank fast, as the Aggies ended the game with an aggressive 25–1 run.

GREATEST COACH QUOTES

"What you are as a person is far more important than what you are as a basketball player." —JOHN WOODEN, UCLA COACH

"Concentration and mental toughness are the margins of victory." —BILL RUSSELL, CELTICS PLAYER/COACH

"Basketball is a beautiful game when the five players on the court play with one heartbeat." —DEAN SMITH, UNC COACH

"There are only two options regarding commitment. You're either in or you're out. There's no such thing as life in between." —PAT RILEY, NBA COACH AND EXECUTIVE

"Basketball is a team sport. If you're into individual things, take up tennis!" —TARA VANDERVEER, STANFORD COACH

"A person really doesn't become whole, until he becomes a part of something that's bigger than himself." —JIM VALVANO, NC STATE COACH

"You can't always be the most talented person in the room, but you can be the most competitive." —PAT SUMMITT, TENNESSEE COACH

Penn junior forward Michelle Nwokedi (15 points and 7 rebounds) and senior center Sydney Stipanovich (20 points) did their best early on to help their team advance in the tournament, but Texas A&M junior center Khaalia Hillsman (27 points) and sophomore forward Anriel Howard (16 rebounds) just weren't having it.

The 63–61 fourth-quarter comeback victory was the biggest turnaround in NCAA Women's history. After the game, Coach Blair proudly proclaimed, "The game is never over at A&M until we decide it's over." Sounds like a coach who believed in his players, not just early on, but all the way through.

THE RETURN OF THE MIGHTY ZO

A HALL OF FAME CENTER BATTLES A RARE KIDNEY DISORDER

Known simply as "Zo," **ALONZO MOURNING** is one of the greatest defenders in the history of the game. Before stars like Dwyane Wade, Bam Adebayo, and Jimmy Butler laced up their sneakers for the Heat, Zo was the hoops king of Miami. But in 2000, the seven-time All-Star center was diagnosed with a condition called glomerulosclerosis. It involves scarring of the blood vessels in the kidneys. Zo needed an organ donor to give him a new kidney, and his phenomenal career seemed over.

Mourning had been a golden-boy superstar player since middle school in his hometown of Chesapeake, Virginia. Nearly every college team recruited him after an almost perfect high

school career. He chose to play at Georgetown University under legendary coach John Thompson. After he graduated, the Charlotte Hornets selected him as the second overall pick in the 1992 NBA Draft. Zo played only three seasons with Charlotte but quickly solidified himself as one of the best young defenders in the league. He was then traded to the Miami Heat.

In the seven years that he spent balling for the Heat, Zo became a bona fide superstar. The NBA crowned him the Defensive Player of the Year back-to-back in 1999 and 2000, and he became a perennial All-Star while he played in Miami. He was also a member of the 2000 USA Olympic gold medal team, along with his Heat teammate Tim Hardaway.

After winning gold at the Sydney Olympics, Mourning was diagnosed with glomerulosclerosis. The condition worsened over the next couple of years, and, in 2003, he announced his retirement from the NBA. Meanwhile, he searched for someone who could donate one of their two kidneys. Hall of Fame Knicks center Patrick Ewing, Zo's good friend and on-court rival, offered to donate one of his. But someone else stepped up, too—a month later, doctors successfully transplanted a kidney from Zo's cousin, Jason Cooper.

Mourning then began his lengthy recovery. Not many people thought he'd play another NBA game—but Zo knew he would. After missing the entire 2002–03 season, he signed with the New Jersey

Nets and triumphantly made it back onto the court. He didn't play many games for the next couple of seasons, but in 2005, my man went back to the place that had made him a star: Miami. With the Heat, he played an invaluable role as a backup center and team leader.

In Miami, Mourning played limited minutes per night to preserve his strength and maximize his effectiveness. Even still, he remained one of the league leaders in blocks. Zo could swat the ball like he was batting away tennis balls at Wimbledon. In 2005–06, he backed up MVP center Shaquille O'Neal, and the Heat won the Eastern Conference. They then beat the Dallas Mavericks in the Finals to become the NBA Champs.

Zo was finally a champion. Talk about a huge source of inspiration for just about anyone facing adversity. Mourning called it quits on his fifteen-year career in 2009. That year he became the first player in the team's history to have his jersey number, 33,

retired. But Mourning wasn't quite done with basketball—or winning. He has served in the front office as the Vice President of Player Programs for the Heat since 2009, winning two more championship rings in that role. Best of all, he was inducted into the Hall of Fame in 2014.

Way to go, Zo!

WHEN THE GAME IS OVER

INTERESTING CAREERS AFTER RETIRING FROM BASKETBALL

PLAYER	HOOPS CAREER		POST-HOOPS CAREER
JALEN ROSE	NBA	13 seasons	ESPN analyst
TRACY MCGRADY	NBA	15 seasons	Pro baseball pitcher
RENEE MONTGOMERY	WNBA	11 seasons	Atlanta Dream co-owner
RONY SEIKALY	NBA	11 seasons	Music producer, DJ
BILL BRADLEY	NBA	10 seasons	US senator
ANGEL McCOUGHTRY	WNBA	13 seasons	Ice cream shop owner
MICHAEL JORDAN	NBA	15 seasons	Charlotte Hornets owner
LISA LESLIE	WNBA	12 seasons	Sports commentator/actor
TIM DUNCAN	NBA	19 seasons	MMA fighter
BRYANT REEVES	NBA	6 seasons	Cattle rancher

THE 0.1-PERCENT CHANCE WINNERS

THE MOST DRAMATIC NCAA TOURNAMENT COMEBACK EVER

Sometimes it just takes one sweet, textbook-perfect jumper to motivate the troops and set off the comeback.

On March 18, 2018, the **NEVADA WOLF PACK** were hanging on by a skinny thread in the second half of a second-round NCAA tournament game in Nashville, Tennessee. The Pack trailed the slightly favored **CINCINNATI BEARCATS** by 12 points at halftime. At the start of the second half, Cincy turned up the pressure even more as their lead ballooned to 22 points. Now they were really starting to crush the Wolf Pack's dreams of returning to the Sweet Sixteen round, which they hadn't reached in fourteen years. With 11 minutes left in the game, the score was an abysmal 65–43.

But 11 minutes is a big enough chunk of time if you believe in yourself—and maybe in miracles, too.

Nevada had a much smaller team than Cincinnati, but they did have three seniors on their roster. When all the guys huddled in those final 11 minutes, they vowed not to let their elder statesmen finish their college careers with a tough loss. Plus, they had a little extra motivation to lean on: Before the game, they found out that Bearcat "Sweet Sixteen" T-shirts and gear were already for sale, like Cincy just *knew* Nevada would lose. No way!

Though his team was outsized, head coach Eric Musselman decided to use the Wolf Pack's quickness to their advantage. The team began to play at a higher tempo and then switched to a full-court, man-to-man, trap-style of defense. This means pressuring the ball handler aggressively, and sometimes double-teaming him until he mishandles the ball. And you know what? It worked. With only 11:34 left in the game, Cincy was up by 22 and had a 99.9 percent statistical chance of winning. But incredibly, Nevada's odds began to increase sharply.

Junior forward CODY MARTIN triggered the comeback with a beautiful midrange jumper. All of a sudden, the floodgates opened for a team that had been left for dead. A swift 10–0 run, led by the MARTIN TWINS (Cody and Caleb) and senior captain KENDALL STEPHENS, gave the Pack much-needed confidence.

They kept pressuring Cincy to take ugly, ill-advised shots. Before long, the Bearcats were in foul trouble, and their leading scorers started heading for the bench. The Pack piled on their opponents' misfortunes, and before you knew it, the score was close at 73–68 with 2:09 remaining.

With less than a minute left in the game and the score now 73–70, Caleb hit a critical trey and tied it up—FINALLY! The Wolf Pack mustered up another strong defensive press, got the ball back, and then the other twin, Cody, sank a jumper to take the lead. After a Bearcat miss, guard Josh Hall plucked the rebound, and with 13 seconds left on the clock, he hit a heavenly floating shot that froze the crowd in the Bridgestone Arena. With that basket, Nevada edged out a bonkers 75–73 win over Cincinnati.

There is your miracle. Just goes to show you that if you keep battling, keep pushing forward, and maybe even change up your original game plan, that sliver of a possibility may be all you need for victory.

REGGIE WRECKS THE KNICKS

8 POINTS IN 8.9 SECONDS

Before we get into the soul-snatching, crowd-silencing comeback at Madison Square Garden in New York City on the evening of May 15, 1995, there are a few things that you need to know about **REGGIE MILLER**:

★ He was the eleventh pick in the 1987 NBA Draft by the Indiana Pacers.

★ He is from Riverside, California, and still holds tons of college records at UCLA.

★ He is a five-time NBA All-Star, Olympic gold medalist, Hall of Famer, and one of the *deadliest* three-point shooters ever (fourth all-time with 2,560 total).

Okay, now that we've got those important stats out of the way, this is what went down that night in Game 1 of the Eastern Conference Semifinals between the Indiana Pacers and the New York Knicks. With the score 105–99, the Knicks had a solid 6-point lead with only 18.7 seconds left in the game. It was important for New York to assert themselves and start the series off right. You always want to win at home, right? The Knicks were tough—they usually left their opponents battered and bruised at the end of games, especially with their leader, center PATRICK EWING, at the helm. Everything seemed in control—that is, until Reggie Miller went bananas....

First, the Pacers' star sharpshooter caught a half-court pass. Reggie quickly launched one of his beautiful arching treys. *Butter.* The clock read 16.4 seconds, and the score was now 105–102. Uh-oh. Iconic movie director Spike Lee, a die-hard Knicks fan who had been jawing with Reggie throughout the game, was standing courtside and looked visibly distraught. On the next play, Knicks forward Anthony Mason attempted an inbound pass to guard Greg Anthony, but Greg slipped! Reggie jumped in front of him, dribbled back behind the three-point line, and drained another triple. Two threes in three seconds!

Spike and thousands of Knicks fans believed that Reggie shoved Anthony to the floor. But what could they do? No foul was called. The score was now tied with 13.2 seconds left in the game.

Then Knicks guard John Starks caught an inbound pass but was fouled immediately. Here's where things got *really* crazy. Starks, who was usually an automatic bucket at the free throw line, missed both shots. The second shot bounced around the rim, Patrick Ewing grabbed the rebound but missed the putback, and lanky Reggie snatched the rock for a clutch board. He was fouled immediately after the rebound, went to the line, and sank both of his shots. In the extra-loud, hostile Madison Square Garden environment, Reggie showed ice-cold concentration and will to win. Indiana went up 107–105, the clock hit zero, and the Pacers were victorious.

Reggie finished the game with the same point total as the number he wore on his jersey: 31. Big players show up in big games. Reggie was a big-time trash-talker on the court—to the opposing players, fans, and especially Spike Lee. But hey, he could always back it up, no matter how much time remained on the clock. His 8 points in 8.9 seconds remains a truly phenomenal playoff feat.

END OF REGULATION

Well, that's a wrap, y'all. Like a Finals Game 7, all tied up, 0.9 seconds left on the clock, with the ball launched from the three-point line and hurling in slow motion toward the net. And guess who took the shot? Ice-cold Steph Curry.

It's all over. Game. Over.

I hope you've picked up a lot of basketball facts that you can carry around in your head to share with friends, family, and just about anybody who will listen. I mean, who else is going to tell your buddies about the greatness of Pat Summitt in such regal and precise detail as you? Or who can share the groundbreaking tales of Dr. J, the New York Rens, and George Mikan? And you'll probably wanna tell everybody about the time Blake Griffin leaped over a whole car, or how the UConn women's basketball squad went on a four-season winning streak—FOUR SEASONS!

The game has evolved so much since Dr. Naismith and Coach Abbott wrote the rules more than a century ago. It's increasingly becoming an international phenomenon, too, even rivaling the popularity of soccer—excuse me, fútbol. But one thing stays constant: Throughout its rich history, basketball has tied together culture, heritage, and the advancement of many marginalized people, like Black and female players. Hopefully the sport will continue to evolve, be more inclusive of people of all backgrounds, and create even more global change agents—both on and off the court.

And who knows, you might be up next. Sure, you could be the next superstar point guard or the first woman head coach of an NBA team. But now you have the information to make you hungrier to learn even more about the game's origins, its key players, and its potential to change the world.

So go forth, you expert of roundball; you genius of hoops; you oracle of hardwood, dirt, and concrete courts (shout-out to the Rucker!). You are the chosen one. You're the maestro they'll seek out when hard-to-find basketball truth is needed. It will be you who they'll bow to for one glorious reason alone: YOU GOT GAME.

Always have. Always will. Peace.

TIPS & RESOURCES

Abdul-Jabbar, Kareem. *Becoming Kareem: Growing Up On and Off the Court.* Little, Brown. 2017.

Alexander, Kwame. *The Playbook: 52 Rules to Aim, Shoot, and Score in This Game Called Life.* Clarion Books. 2017.

Berglund, Bruce. *Basketball GOATs: The Greatest Athletes of All Time.* Capstone. 2022.

Bryant, Howard. *Legends: The Best Players, Games, and Teams in Basketball.* Puffin Books. 2017.

Buckley, James, Jr. *It's a Numbers Game! Basketball: The Math Behind the Perfect Bounce Pass, the Buzzer-Beating Bank Shot, and So Much More!* National Geographic Kids. 2020.

Coy, John. *Hoop Genius: How a Desperate Teacher and a Rowdy Gym Class Invented Basketball.* Carolrhoda Books. 2013.

Donne, Elena Delle. *My Shot: Balancing It All and Standing Tall.* Simon & Schuster Books for Young Readers. 2018.

Schaller, Bob. *The Everything Kids' Basketball Book: A Guide to Your Favorite Players and Teams—and Tips on Playing Like a Pro.* 5th ed. Everything. 2021.

KNOW YOUR STUFF WITH THESE SITES

NAISMITH MEMORIAL BASKETBALL HALL OF FAME hoophall.com

BASKETBALL REFERENCE basketball-reference.com

BLACK FIVES FOUNDATION blackfives.org

THE OFFICIAL SITE OF THE NATIONAL BASKETBALL ASSOCIATION nba.com

WOMEN'S BASKETBALL HALL OF FAME wbhof.com

GLOSSARY

- -

ABA: The American Basketball Association was a professional men's league from 1967 to 1976.

ALL-AMERICAN: An amateur player (high school or college player) whom the media decides is among the best in the nation.

ALL-STAR: An All-Star is the player in each position that fans, media, and other players decide is the best. In the NBA, once the All-Stars are selected, two player-captains pick their squads to play against each other in the All-Star Game.

ALLEY-OOP: An alley-oop is an attacking play that involves two players: One passes the ball, while the other jumps and dunks before landing.

ASSIST: The final pass that leads to a basket.

BACKBOARD: The flat board behind the hoop.

BALL-HANDLING/HANDLES: Dribbling and ball-control skills.

BARNSTORMING: When teams like the Harlem Globetrotters travel to play matches on the road. These games happen outside of an official league. .

BASELINE: The baseline runs the width of the court behind the hoop.

BIG MAN/BIG: A position also known as the center. Bigs are usually the tallest players.

BLOCK: When a defensive player blocks another player's shot by intercepting the ball while it is mid-flight.

BLUE-BLOOD TEAM: College basketball programs that are known for being really successful, like Duke, North Carolina, Kansas, and Kentucky.

CENTER: One of the five basketball positions. The center is usually the tallest on the team, and they play around the basket on both offense and defense.

CHARITY STRIPE: A nickname for the free throw line.

CROSSOVER: A move where the player quickly dribbles the ball from one hand to the other to change directions.

DIME/DISH: A nickname for an assist.

DOUBLE TEAM: A defensive strategy in which two players guard one attacking player.

DPOY: Stands for the Defensive Player of the Year award.

DRAFT: In a draft, professional teams take turns selecting from a pool of rookie or international players. Drafts occur at the end of each season.

DYNASTY: A team that wins multiple championships and dominates the competition over many seasons.

EXPANSION DRAFT: When the NBA decides to create a new team, an expansion draft allows the team to fill its roster from players already in the league.

EXPANSION TEAM: A new team in the league, usually created in a city that doesn't already have a team.

FAST BREAK: A strategy where the team rushes the ball up the court while the defense is still out of position.

FRONT OFFICE: The people who work for a team making business and roster decisions—including the owner, general manager, and other operations.

FULL-COURT PRESS: A playing style where defenders press for the full length of the court, instead of standing near the basket.

GENERAL MANAGER: The front office executive responsible for building and maintaining a team's roster, from trading players to signing free agents.

GLASS: Also known as the backboard.

HOOK/SKYHOOK: A shot in which a player turned sideways to the basket uses one hand to arc the ball into the hoop.

HOOPER: A great basketball player.

HOPS: A player's jumping ability. If you've got "great hops," for instance, you can jump extremely high to grab rebounds, dunk, or shoot over defenders.

INBOUND PASS: A pass coming from out of court that restarts game play.

INTRAMURAL LEAGUE: A league made up of teams from within a school or other institution.

IVY LEAGUE: An athletic conference featuring eight prestigious colleges.

LARRY O'BRIEN TROPHY: The trophy awarded to the team that wins the NBA Finals.

MAN-TO-MAN DEFENSE: A strategy where each player is in charge of tracking and defending one player on the other team.

MVP: Stands for Most Valuable Player. It is an award given to one player per year for their outstanding performance throughout the season.

NAISMITH MEMORIAL BASKETBALL HALL OF FAME: A museum and hall of fame dedicated to celebrating the history of the game and its greatest players.

NBA: Stands for the National Basketball Association. The NBA is the world's top men's professional basketball league.

NCAA: Stands for National Collegiate Athletic Association. The NCAA is the organization that regulates college athletics across the United States and Canada.

PAINTED AREA: The area between the free throw line and the hoop. Also called "the paint" or "the key," it is usually painted with the home team's colors.

POINT GUARD: One of the five basketball positions. A point guard is usually the team's best ball handler and passer.

POWER FORWARD: One of the five basketball positions. A power forward is similar in build to a center but focuses more on shooting from both inside and outside of the paint.

POWERHOUSE COLLEGE: A college with a well-known, successful basketball program.

PUTBACK: When a shot misses and another offensive player gets the ball off the rebound and immediately puts it back in the hoop, all in one motion.

ROCK: Slang for the ball.

ROLE PLAYER: A player who comes off the bench. They're not superstars but are still crucial to the success of the team.

ROOKIE OF THE YEAR: An award given to the best first-year player each season.

RUN-AND-GUN OFFENSE: A fast-paced style of play where the team moves the ball forward as quickly as possible, often leading to high-scoring games.

SEMIPRO PLAYERS: Basketball players who don't play full-time but still get paid for playing in smaller or minor leagues.

SHOOTING GUARD: One of the five basketball positions. A shooting guard specializes in baskets from around the three-point line.

SLAM DUNK: A shot where the player jumps and drives the ball right into the hoop. Some famous types of dunks include the windmill, reverse and between the legs.

SMALL FORWARD: Small forwards are the most versatile of the five positions. They are usually agile and do a little bit of everything on the court.

STRETCHING THE FLOOR: When a player can shoot threes as well as in the paint, they draw defenders out, allowing more space for teammates to attack the basket.

TRAP DEFENSE: Where two defensive players double-team an attacking player who is handling the ball.

THREE-PEAT: A term for winning three championships in a row.

TREY: Slang for a three-pointer.

WING: The outer section of the court along the sidelines.

WINNING PERCENTAGE: A common statistic that shows what fraction of games played that a team (or individual) has won.

WNBA: Stands for the Women's National Basketball Association. The WNBA is the world's top women's professional basketball league.

ABOUT THE AUTHOR

DERRICK BARNES is the author of *Who Got Game?: Baseball* and is a National Book Award Finalist for his graphic novel *Victory. Stand!: Raising My Fist for Justice*. Derrick is the winner of the Ezra Jack Keats Award, a Newbery Honor, and the YALSA Excellence In Young Adult Non Fiction Award and is a two-time Coretta Scott King Honoree and two-time Kirkus Prize for Young Readers recipient. He is also the author of *Crown: An Ode to the Fresh Cut* and three New York Times bestsellers: *The King of Kindergarten*, *The Queen of Kindergarten*, and *I Am Every Good Thing*. Derrick lives in Charlotte, North Carolina, with his wife and four sons.

ABOUT THE ILLUSTRATOR

JEZ TUYA is a children's book illustrator based in Wellington, New Zealand. Notable past clients include Walker Books, Andersen Press, Nosy Crow, and Albert Whitman and Company. He is married to Jane, and papa to Orla and Ethan. When he isn't making art in the studio, he enjoys spending time outdoors or watching movies with his lovely wife.